Photo by Carol Lazar

JAMES K. FEIBLEMAN was until 1969 Chairman and Professor of Philosophy at Tulane University where he has taught philosophy since 1942; he has also been Special Lecturer in the Department of Psychiatry at Louisiana State University Medical School from 1958 to 1967. In 1975-76 he was Bingham Professor of Philosophy at the University of Louisville, where in 1976 he was awarded the honorary degree of Doctor of Humane Letters, and in 1977 Doctor of Laws by Tulane University. More than 160 of his articles have appeared in journals of philosophy, psychiatry, education, and sociology, and in popular magazines. He was a founder in 1952 of the annual, *Tulane Studies in Philosophy*, and for many years its editor. Many of his writings have been translated into foreign languages. He is past president of the Peirce Society and the New Orleans Academy of Sciences, and is an honorary Phi Beta Kappa. Among his books are: *Understanding Philosophy; Understanding Civilizations; Understanding Oriental Philosophy; The Reach of Politics: A New Look at Government; In Praise of Comedy; The Quiet Rebellion: The Making and Meaning of the Arts;* and his autobiography *The Way of a Man.*

Books by James K. Feibleman

DEATH OF THE GOD IN MEXICO
CHRISTIANITY, COMMUNISM AND THE IDEAL SOCIETY
IN PRAISE OF COMEDY
POSITIVE DEMOCRACY
THE MARGITIST
THE THEORY OF HUMAN CULTURE
THE REVIVAL OF REALISM
AN INTRODUCTION TO PEIRCE'S PHILOSOPHY
JOURNEY TO THE COASTAL MARSH
THE LONG HABIT
AESTHETICS
ONTOLOGY
PHILOSOPHERS LEAD SHELTERED LIVES
TREMBLING PRAIRIE
THE DARK BIFOCALS
THE INSTITUTIONS OF SOCIETY
THE PIOUS SCIENTIST
INSIDE THE GREAT MIRROR
RELIGIOUS PLATONISM
FOUNDATIONS OF EMPIRICISM
BIOSOCIAL FACTORS IN MENTAL ILLNESS
MANKIND BEHAVING
THE TWO-STORY WORLD
MORAL STRATEGY
GREAT APRIL
THE REACH OF POLITICS
THE WAY OF A MAN
THE NEW MATERIALISM
SCIENTIFIC METHOD
THE QUIET REBELLION
UNDERSTANDING PHILOSOPHY
COLLECTED POEMS
THE STAGES OF HUMAN LIFE
UNDERSTANDING CIVILIZATIONS
UNDERSTANDING ORIENTAL PHILOSOPHY
ADAPTIVE KNOWING

Co-Author of

SCIENCE AND THE SPIRIT OF MAN
THE UNLIMITED COMMUNITY
WHAT SCIENCE REALLY MEANS

Understanding Human Nature

A Popular Guide to the Effects of Technology on Man and His Behavior

JAMES K. FEIBLEMAN

HORIZON PRESS  New York

Copyright© 1977 by James K. Feibleman
Library of Congress Catalog Card No.: 77-77126
ISBN: 0-8180-1322-2
Manufactured in the United States of America

All things are the measures of man

Things are in the saddle,
And ride mankind.
                    — R. W. Emerson,
"Ode Inscribed to W. H. Channing"

Great is the power of power steering
                    — Anonymous

Contents

Contents

Understanding
Human
Nature

Chapter I
Old Topic, New Problems

When I began the writing of this book I had no idea what I was letting myself in for. Most of us think we know what human nature is, and many treatises have been written on the authors' assumptions that they were merely repeating common knowledge.

There has been a revolution in ideas concerning human nature extending well beyond established notions, a revolution brought about by what has been described as "the information explosion." The term is not an exaggeration; many of our oldest beliefs have been swept away and even our common sense is challenged.

A man or a woman who is confined to ordinary experience these days is like a blind prizefighter lashing out in the darkness without knowing where the blows that hit him are coming from. (As a matter of fact they are coming from the smallest of bacteria inside the body as well as from the largest of star systems in outer space.)

Let's consider some of the established "truths" that we have had to give up: For a long time it has been supposed that "what goes up must come down," that "nature abhors a vacuum," and that "human nature never changes."

Is it true any longer that "what goes up must down down"? The Pioneer 10 spacecraft was launched March 3, 1972 from Cape Kennedy, programmed to explore the environment of Jupiter after orbiting Mars, and then, assisted by Jupiter's gravity, to leave the Solar System and never to return. It went up; it will not come down.

How about "nature's abhorrence of a vacuum"? Garrett Birkhoff in his study of hydrodynamics has ascertained that "nature's abhorrence of a vacuum is limited to thirty-five feet of water" because of some daily variation.

What about the saying that "human nature never changes"? Yes; and no. How it has changed, and to what extent, we shall find out in the following pages, and the discovery may come as a complete and stunning surprise. For we are not at all like what we thought we were. In place of the old conceptions of human nature we have many new theories and a multitude of recently discovered facts to support them.

The term, "human nature", does not mean the same thing to everyone. Sometimes it means the quirks and peculiarities of the individual, as when we say of one who contradicts his principles by his actions, "that is human nature." Sometimes it means the uniformity and reliability of all human conduct and its typical consequences.

It is this last meaning that I shall follow here. Accordingly, there is nothing in this book about the abnormal personality or about what is unusual in human life, only about ordinary people. I have not discussed illnesses of any sort; nor deviations from the normal, nor the personality, the unique quality by means of which one differs from others. I have tried to picture the human situation as it is found in any society — wherever, in fact, there are men and women. In short, I have sought to discover and explain the meaning of the usual.

The classical treatment of the topic is best exemplified by the eighteenth century *Treatise* of David Hume. He was chiefly concerned with thought: how ideas arise from sense impressions, and how impossible it is to know anything with certainty about the external world. Human nature for him exists locked up in the mind where it can be studied separately.

Yet Hume's doubt about our ability to know anything that takes place on the outside was contradicted, as he himself noted, by the very fact that actions occur. He had been talking exclusively in terms of consciousness, and so when he recognized that in any action the human individual is in direct physical contact with material things, it upset his theory.

John Dewey two centuries later did include the interplay between man and the environment in his understanding of human nature. But he saw both as mediated by the mind, and so he too did not get very far out of the charmed mental circle. He did not notice the cultural effects on man of the material alterations in his environment.

Sociology suggests itself in this connection, but the sociologists, it seems to me, are no help in the effort to understand human nature because they treat of behavior as though it takes place in a vacuum. Man does not just behave, he behaves *about* something, usually a material object of some sort, often one he has made for himself. Sociologists do not take sufficiently into account the objects which occasion the behavior and so need to be considered in the explanation of it.

On the mention of *"material* objects" the name one is likely to think of is Karl Marx. Marxism is a kind of materialism, but it is not the only kind and is in fact far from what I mean by the term. Marx's materialism is out of date. As Marx himself insisted, it depended upon the mode of production. The automated factories and the labor unions have changed things a great deal since Marx's day, so much so that what he had to say about it no longer applies.

One other, and newer, approach, introduced under the name of ethology, has been defined as the study of the relations between organisms and their environment. It has been pursued chiefly in the case of lower animals, but applies to human animals as well.

The prospect of considering man in relation to his environment is a comparatively new one. It discloses a peculiarity which has not been sufficiently examined: man in the course of his adaptations has modified nature.

If man is historically a product of his environment and continually changed by it, then he can be considered only in interactions with it. Any adequate description of human nature must include an account of how with his fellows he has transformed his world and consequently himself; not only what he has done to it but what as a result it does to him.

The first reaction of the child when he looks about him is wonder; if a grown man continues to wonder in the pauses that occur in his daily life, it is only the natural outcome of his awareness that he exists. Curiosity is responsible for his inquiry into the causes of that existence. The attempt to satisfy it begins in his immediate neighborhood, and radiates outward in ever-increasing circles until it includes all of his other needs.

I start with the study of human motivation before trying to see where man's pursuit of his needs has led him. What is it that makes people do what they do? The first answer lies in their efforts to maintain themselves, to stay alive. But the search will not end there.

When I say "human nature" I mean the single individual with all his capacities and limitations; but where do his boundaries end? With his family and his properties? With his society and its possessions? With his ambition and its global reaches?

To answer these questions it is necessary first to examine the natural world, and then to concentrate on that portion of it which man has been able to change by using his material tools. The search will take us next into the social institutions by which such artifacts have had to be managed; next into nations; and finally into the international scene.

For culture is indivisible: to recognize the meaning of any one part of man's endeavor involves tracing it to all the others. With this fact as guide we may arrive at an understanding of human nature, which begins with the individual and ends with the largest and most enduring of human constructions — civilization itself.

It remains only to observe how few people are concerned with truth unless it favors one cause or another and seems to come down on the side of the interests of some special group. Truth serves no one in particular, and ought to be a precious common possession. If it is not so regarded that can be only because we do not know our own good. The unaffiliated truth should stand alone as a global aim. In the conduct of practical affairs there are no truths and no falsehoods, only half-truths which are by definition half-false. It is important to remember, however, that "half-truths" are half true, and we live by them.

Chapter II
The Total Environment

The human species is tied to its environment more intimately than is commonly recognized. Those individuals who can make use of the materials around them, survive; those who cannot, perish. Since the characteristics of a population approximate closely to external conditions, we shall make a short detour through the world that man inhabits before taking a closer look at him.

Man in the Middle

Man occupies a middle place in nature. He is an object of medium size, for there are as many things smaller as there are larger.

First let us take the direction toward the smaller objects.

Beginning with the entire man, we find that he is composed of organs: heart, lungs, stomach, kidney and the like. All these in their turn are composed of cells. Without going into too many details (for there are many different kinds of cells) let us say that cells are composed of molecules — complex combinations of proteins, fats and carbohydrates, vitamins, salts, and enzymes.

There are very small organisms, such as bacteria and the even smaller viruses. Single molecules are composed of atoms, the atoms composed of electrons, protons, and many other particles similar in size. Below these are the quarks, and below the quarks no one has gone — yet.

Beginning once again with the entire man and looking toward the larger objects we find that he stands on the surface of the earth as, together with the other planets, it revolves around the sun in an outside spiral arm of the Galaxy. Next in size are the millions of other suns and planets. Beyond the Galaxy there are millions of other galaxies of approximately the same size though differing somewhat in shape.

Man is affected by everything in nature on both sides of him, the smaller as well as the larger, and from the inside as well as the outside. He is affected for instance by bacteria on the inside and by gravitation and other radiation on the outside.

Nature is all of a piece. The same kind of atoms that are found in all organisms, including man, are found also in the planets and stars and interstellar gases. If I put together what is known about both worlds, the smaller and the larger, you will see that it constitutes a single great material system.

In recent centuries we have learned a lot about matter. Before then it hardly counted, since it was believed to consist in bits of inert stuff having no properties except its physical dimensions. Now, thanks to the discoveries of modern physics, all that has been changed. We know better. We have come to recognize that matter is complex, infinitely divisible, averagely distributed, rare, uniform, and interconvertible with energy.

There are many places in the universe where there is matter without life but none where there is life without matter. Most matter is made of fire, like the stars, but there are also quiet corners, like the planets, where life sometimes emerges. Man exists in one quiet corner in a universe of exploding stars and colliding galaxies, but even that corner is not always so quiet if you count the earthquakes, volcanos, hurricanes, tornados, and extremes of heat and cold.

Comparatively speaking, man is a small organism and he lives in a large world. Light, moving at approximately 186,000 miles per second, has to travel from the Andromeda Galaxy, the nearest and brightest of the galaxies, for two million years before it reaches us. Man's environment is part of that world. He is linked to it through his connections with all living things and also with the winds of the sky and the rocks of the earth. He lives on the surface of it, surrounded by oceans of water, at the bottom of a sea of gas, called air, while deriving his energy from plants which in turn get theirs from sunlight. He cannot survive very far above that surface and he cannot penetrate very far below it.

The requirements of life call for narrow confines indeed, for he must cling to a dead planet while it makes endless orbits of a star. This is the scene where man first emerged as a species and where he continues to maintain his existence.

We will be interested more particularly in that small segment of the material world with which man comes into contact. An individual glancing about him would never suspect the complexity of his surroundings. It has taken many investigators working in the sciences for centuries to bring us even a glimpse of the truth.

Levels of Organization in Nature

There is only one natural world, but it falls into divisions of its own. Nature — the natural world — is, like a layer cake or an office building, a vertical structure containing a number of horizontal levels, each with is own characteristics but depending upon all those under it.

At the bottom, and supporting all the others, are the physical levels. The material things and the forms of energy found here are very small. There are three forms of energy at the physical level: electromagnetic, gravitational and nuclear.

This in brief is the nature of the physical world studied by the physical scientists, who design and conduct experiments to learn about it. They discovered its properties, but of course the physical world was here before they were — some 13 billion years before.

The physical level supports all the others and all the constituents remain. The next level above in the order of complexity is the chemical, and it is composed of molecules. The chemical elements and their compounds are familiar to us because we can see and feel them in naturally occurring substances under ordinary circumstances — water and air for instance. Actually, there is an enormous range of chemical elements all the way from the single atom of hydrogen to the 92 atoms of uranium, with some rarer elements beyond that containing even more atoms. The energy to be found at this level is called valence, and it consists in the combining power of the molecules.

Scientifically advanced countries have produced a whole chemical industry, including factories which make the nitrogen used by farmers to increase the fertility of the soil, and others which make artificial fibers. Some of the chemical materials are found in their native state and have only to be processed—sulphur for example.

The next level above the chemical is the biological, perhaps a more familiar one to most people. The energy at this level is called life, and it consists in a certain measure of self-determination. Organisms are capable of arranging for their own growth, self-repair and reproduction.

Some organisms — the human, for example — have a high degree of self-awareness, called mind or consciousness, and this level is represented by the whole human organism. Energy here is called "spirit." Many animals experience a consciousness of sorts but probably not a consciousness of themselves, not self-consciousness. After all, we are human beings, and we respond to the demands and opportunities available to us as organisms.

Finally, there is a top level which consists in collections of individual organisms inter-related with material artifacts in still another organization: the social or cultural. It too has its own quality, the ethos, a quality peculiar to long-standing social organizations such as nations, entire cultures and even civilizations.

That all the levels belong together can be seen from some of the relations which hold between them; for example, the organizations at each level organize the one below and add one new quality. That is why it is impossible to reduce anything to its lowest level. Every material thing contains the properties of the lowest level but also all the properties of every level to which it belongs. It belongs, properly speaking, to its highest level but the higher always depends on the lower: destroy the lower and you do away at the same time with the higher.

Where does man fit into this picture of the world of levels? We can claim for him that he belongs to all the levels but chiefly to the social or cultural. For he has a *physical* body composed of physical elements, he has a *biological* organism and possesses a *psychological* consciousness, yes, but above all he is a member of a *culture* and could not survive long without its society or its artifacts any more than without his physical body, chemical constituents, animal organism, or consciousness.

Individual man is aware not of himself first but of the world, in the middle of which he finds oddly enough that there is himself. No wonder that he fits so neatly into his environment. He is a part of it, and he interacts continually with it in ways which affect them both. He has complex needs and he must find satisfactions for them in a complex environment in which elements from all the levels of organization are mixed together in unpredictable ways.

Two Extensions: The Small and The Large

Let us suppose that a man out for a walk encounters a tree. He sees it, then he walks up to it and touches its trunk. He can hear its leaves when they rustled in the wind, he can taste its fruit and smell its flowers, and he can move around it; all common and familiar behavior.

For thousands of years the environment of the individual has been like that; it has confronted him with what was available to him through his unaided senses. The material objects and forces he was aware of were those of a size best suited to him: the things he could see, touch, hear, taste, smell, and move around, were those he could best understand. His knowledge was limited to them, his common sense, his sanity, and his reason were based on a familiarity with them and with what they could do.

In the last several hundred years, however, this situation has changed radically. For on both sides of this common sense world of ordinary man-sized objects two other worlds have been discovered.

The microscope in the hands of the scientists have brought him close to the world of the small, a world of things the unaided senses cannot detect. We saw something of them already when we looked at atoms, molecules and cells.

Similarly, the telescope has brought him close to the world of the large, again things the unaided senses cannot detect. He must now recognize the existence of other solar systems, the whole of the Milky Way, and many galaxies. His own earth is a small part of the vast system of stars and stellar objects, a fact which was brought home to him when man landed on the moon and sent back pictures of what the earth looked like from there.

The world as it presents itself to his common sense seems far simpler than it is. Almost anything in his environment will serve as an example, consider for instance ordinary sunlight. A simple thing? It contains all the colors and it radiates from the outer atmosphere of the sun, which is a mixture of magnetic field, streaming gas, wave motions and nonthermal particles, in a way still not too well understood by the scientists.

We have noted that gravitation as a world-force affects him also, but it is not the only force that does so; there are cosmic rays that fall regularly on him and his environment. And of course more has been learned about the earth: how the continents that once were connected have drifted apart, how the interior of the earth can move against him through the effects of earthquakes and volcanoes, and how weather changes daily and still more over the centuries.

Little Man, Enormous World

The environment of the individual now is a much broader landscape. It is still composed of middle-sized objects, things within the range of his senses, but reaching out on both sides of that environment and continuous with it are the two extensions of it, the environment of the small on the one side and the environment of the large on the other.

Our knowledge of these adjacent areas is the gift of the experimental scientists with their powerful instruments. They were discovered by the scientists but they do not belong to the scientists, they are extensions of the world. And we must consider them seriously because of their effects. Long before man knew about them they were influencing him. For thousands of years he has been powerless to understand and control many forces at work upon him without his conscious knowledge. The great plagues of the Middle Ages were caused by infections of organisms too small to detect without laboratory assistance. Earthquakes and landslides resulted from the shifting of continents. The new thing is not that such events affect him but that now for the first time he is in a position to do something about them: he prevents epidemics, he seeds clouds with chemicals in order to produce rain, and soon he will be able to predict if not to prevent earthquakes.

Vast changes have occurred in the world man inhabits. He knows now that he lives in a much richer, more extended environment, and as a consequence he finds coping with it a more formidable task. Knowledge increases faster than its applications. Moreover, there is no useless knowledge, only a lag sometimes between its discovery and its uses.

An individual engaged in the ordinary work of the world has to base his procedures on the information furnished by instruments and has to recognize that his world is now composed of connected segments: the small, the ordinary and the large. In terms of such a complex situation how is he to construct a new common sense which will see him through his day-to-day problems?

Man is nothing if not clever. He has noted that while everything changes, the changes take place in recurring patterns. He has seen how important the recurrences were because they have enabled him to predict and even to control events. He has found out, in other words, that they followed regularities which could be formulated as laws.

What he was learning to cope with was the second story of a two-story world. Scientific laws belong to a level different from the events they describe; that is chiefly what is involved. This is not a visionary ideal; it is a stark description of an idea that is used every day. With the discovery of scientific laws there came not only knowledge of the world but also a large measure of control over it. If all members of an organic species are constructed in the same way, then it is possible to learn a lot about them by dissecting a single one in the laboratory. This is as true of men as of mice.

Again, if all matter is interconvertible with energy, then it is possible to unlock the energy in matter according to the invariant laws of particle physics, a theory which led eventually to the nuclear power plants which are being constructed in large numbers in Europe, the Soviet Union and the United States.

Every individual is born with his genes; he is what his ancestors have made him. He inherits his own past and is molded also by circumstances; environment takes over. He lives in and interacts with a mixed collection of things surrounding him in a more or less disorderly fashion. He is continually exposed to stimulation. Reacting to the world, as he does from birth, his involvement with it is a prime condition of his existence; the environment can never be counted out, though some individuals suppose that it can. Those who have been lucky enough to make a seemingly permanent adjustment to a stable environment so that they are left almost entirely to their own devices may find that, despite their best efforts, accidents happen and the entire arrangement is unexpectedly upset.

Chapter III

The Origin of the Individual as a Bundle of Needs

Tools the Man-Maker

Most animals adapt to their environment; few try to change it. There are some exceptions of course: beavers build dams, birds make nests, bees construct hives; but most accommodate themselves to the world as they find it. Species that have managed to maintain themselves in this way almost indefinitely are not uncommon. The Australian lung-fish has survived unchanged for more than 300 million years, the penguin for 40 million, the cockroach for 19 million. None of them has needed to alter the environment in order to survive because each was so well adapted to it.

The case of man is quite different. As an animal species man is a johnny-come-lately. Estimates vary but none places him back very far in time; together with his ancestral species at the most only a few million years, and as he is today, only 40,000. The important thing to notice is that he has developed as a species only by altering his environment in order to render it more suitable to his needs.

A familiar phrase in the accounts of early man is "man the tool maker". It is certainly an accurate one, for stone tools are found with the most primitive remains. But there is more to it than that, for the phrase can be turned around for greater accuracy: "tools the man-maker," for the facts disclose that man developed his large brain and his control over the environment by adapting to the tools he made.

The shift from forest creature to inhabitant of cities took place not more than 10,000 years ago — only yesterday on the evolutionary scale. Evidently value has very little to do with time measured in terms of species survival.

Man, in short, is a product of technology, and would not have come into existence without it. The emergence of his species was due to the invention of tools by an earlier one. Stone tools have been found with hominid remains dating back several million years, long in fact before man himself. Crude implements of bone, wood and stone compelled the assumption of an upright posture which freed the use of the hands, made possible bipedal locomotion, and even accounted for the exchange of cries at a distance.

The first and most primitive human social groups were composed of single families. These may have united to face larger enemies, such as the mastodons. But as a partial division of labor resulted from tool-using, some individuals proved to be more proficient than others in particular crafts and so became warriors, farmers or hunters. Thus the accumulation of tools was eventually responsible for the establishment of villages.

But early men were nomads. They lived on the herds they followed seasonally, moving sometimes daily. Even in our time the Eskimo had to follow the migrations of the caribou. And so being unable to carry very much, they had no opportunities for accumulation.

The nomad can never stop hunting, obtaining food is for him a day-to-day necessity. His life is like that of other animals — a ceaseless search for food. The change came when he got control of his food supply by fencing in and domesticating herds and by cultivating plants, thus making it possible to give up his nomadic existence for a settled community.

Agriculture and animal husbandry gave him control of his immediate environment, so from being its slave he became its master. Storing food enabled him to turn his attention to activities not directly connected with immediate survival. Thus it was that the discovery of a farming economy made civilization possible.

I have a picture in my mind of two elderly nomads seated by an evening fire at the edge of a clearing in the forest and discussing the problems of youth. One of them asked, "Did you hear about my brother's son? I don't know what we are going to do with him. He is not content any longer to follow the reindeer as we and our ancestors have always done. Now he wants to fence them in and grow grasses to feed them."

"What would be the advantage of that?" the other asked.

"He says that then we could keep the things we make because we would not have to carry them every day, and we could build permanent shelters, better ones because we would not have to leave them the next morning."

The first old man only shook his head. "I don't know what the next generation is coming to! Doesn't he know that if his plan was a good one, our grand-fathers would have thought of it long ago? No, the old ways are the best."

How could he know that the young man had been responsible for the start of civilization?

The oldest human remains and even the pre-human types of hominids have been found with crude tools made of bone and stone. Probably there were wood tools, too, but they have long since disappeared. Skills were developed and taught, and men talked to each other about them. The increase in the size of the brain may well have resulted from manual skills and speech. Shaped sounds, and scratches on hard surfaces, representing signs, are also tools; and the more complicated the tools, the larger the human brain. That man exists at all may be the result of some hominid's adaptive responses to the making and using of tools.

By now there is nothing in the environment that man has not changed to suit himself, not the air he breathes nor the ground he walks on. His interactions with the environment have transformed it almost beyond recognition. It is now almost wholly artificial, having been reconstructed by transforming the available materials. He has accomplished this by making and employing tools and other instruments — in a word, artifacts — which may be defined as material objects altered through human efforts in order to make them suitable for human uses. Man now lives in a world of his own devising, composed almost entirely of artifacts: buildings, machines of all sorts, everything in fact from stoves to bulldozers, made in order to compel his environment to serve him better.

We are fully aware that without men there would be no artifacts, but not everyone has noticed that without artifacts there would be no men. Indeed the tables have been turned altogether; man may now be described as artifact-dependent. The life of a civilized man consists for the most part in operating whatever artifacts are suitable to his chosen work. Due to their peculiar construction they can be dealt with only in certain ways. His training for making a living consists in acquiring whatever skills the use of the particular artifacts demand. His is a voluntary servitude, and he responds with learned behavior patterns to whatever the chosen artifacts ask of him. Thus the artificial environment of human culture exercises a selection pressure similar to that of the natural environment in the evolutionary process.

Some artifacts may of course be attended to casually while others require dedication. Let me choose two examples from contemporary life: the airplane pilot, say, and the concert violinist.

Professional skills, occupational hazards and diseases, both exist. A pilot "feels" when things are not right with his aircraft, a violinist can keep his arm turned to an angle that would be impossible for most people. In each case, the man is in a certain sense a captive of the machine he operates. It may be an open question which is serving which, but we do know that man and

machine are involved together in an effort which no one understands completely. Naturally the more civilized men are the more
sophisticated the artifacts they make and use. They continue to do
what they always did: eat and drink, make love, move about, but
thanks to artifacts they do these things much more efficiently and
many of them externally.

Civilization consists in externalization: learning to do outside
the body what had formerly been done only on the inside and in
this way doing it better. Perhaps the most striking instance of
externalization consists in the use of writing in place of speech.
Long before men learned how to write down their thoughts and so
communicate them more widely, they were speaking to each
other, but civilization began with writing, which is an artifact of
thought.

Examples are innumerable: cooking is a form of pre-
digestion, a method of preparing foods that the stomach could not
manage alone. No man can remember all the knowledge that has
accumulated in books, but libraries can. Computers work faster
than individuals. Contraceptives and intra-uterine devices have
made sex safer and therefore more pleasurable. Cars and
airplanes move more quickly than legs, microscopes and telescopes see deeper and farther than eyes.

Looking back at the path man has taken in history, we can
distinguish three distinct stages in the development of artifacts
and three corresponding changes in human behavior. For
thousands, perhaps millions of years the human species was frozen in its first stages of development. Tools made by chipping and
flaking stones dominated the men of the Stone Age, who had to
adapt themselves to their environment and could do little beyond
accepting nature as they found it. This is what has been called an
adaptive response, and the kind of behavior it calls out *stereotyped
behavior,* repeated by generations with few appreciable changes.

That lasted until the coming of settlements and cities, when
in a second stage there was a big jump in the kind of artifacts.
Man, no longer willing to accept raw nature as he found it,
changed it to suit himself. Natural resources are worthless with-

out technology. By using the necessary instruments man learned to transform his environment.

In Sumeria and Egypt, some six thousand years ago, men took the lead in the building of cities, which, we must not forget, are organized collections of artifacts. We might describe their kind of activity as a new kind of adaptation: *constructive behavior.*

Finally, in a third dramatic advance that is no more than a few hundreds years old, the discovery of the scientific method of experiment made it possible to construct artifacts in great numbers and of an unbelievable degree of complexity.

The technological developments of recent decades have outstripped the understanding of the average citizen, who is continually affected by it. Recent examples are: the pipeline switching center operated by the Columbia Gas System in Charleston, West Virginia; the telephone switchboard, the computer, the electron microscope.

More than that, man has learned how to build machines whose only purpose is to run other machines. Thermostats, stabilizers, and a host of other devices do what man no longer needs to do. Entire factories operate with little human assistance. We might call this process *instigative behavior.*

We can understand now that there is a circuit of impulses from the human organism, with its needs and drives, to the environment of artifacts.

In this way it can be fairly said that *civilization is also a kind of intensification.* The basic organic needs of man do not change, do not improve; the means of satisfying them do. The hunger drive has survived intact through the thousands of years from the early cave dweller who was a hunter and gatherer to the contemporary diner with his cafés and restaurants.

In the long period from early man to modern man there has been progress in technology but none in motivation: man has learned to reduce his needs more efficiently, but the needs are the same.

The failure to make progress in motivation when everything else has improved is one of the terrifying facts of human existence.

Two of the conflicting motives of individual are to help his neighbors and to hurt them. And of course each has always had artifacts to match. The primitive tribe had its medicine man with his herbs and incantations whose aim was to heal, and the warrior with bow and arrow whose aim was to kill. Modern counterparts are doctors with their hospitals, and soldiers with nuclear weapons. The means have been greatly improved in efficiency, the ends are exactly the same.

Man has provided for himself a new and almost wholly artificial environment. We call it *culture*, which may be defined as the works of man and their effects (including of course, their effects on man).

Man Observed

We have seen something of how the world that man inhabits is constructed, now we shall look at what he has to do to survive in it. (I am of course using the generic term "man" to denote man and woman.)

The inquiry will take us into the broad area of human motives: needs, drives, emotions. It will lead to an examination of the consequences of such needs and drives, which do not stop until they have resulted in the whole of culture and civilization.

Man is a changing individual who grew to maturity while under the influences of genetic inheritance and immediate environment, forces that helped to shape him from both inside and outside. To sort out how much of each is involved is all but impossible.

He has to work hard just to maintain himself. For this task he comes equipped with three capacities: he can think, he can feel, and he can act, and he is able to work endless variations on all three. Equipped with a complex set of organs he has the task of coping with a complex environment.

Let us suppose that an individual takes a trip in his car near a big city and looks at what he passes on the way — a produce farm, most likely, and a cattle ranch, possibly fruit trees, a chemical plant, an oil refinery, a factory, a modern hospital, a university —.

All of which arose as responses to his needs. How much does he understand of what goes on in them? Farming, like industry and college teaching, is a special technical business conducted by professionals trained for what they are doing. For the first time in history most people do not understand their own civilization or what is known about the universe surrounding it.

Most of man's needs are animal needs, but he has others. He needs food and drink, a mate, comfort, protection from the weather and from enemies, but he also needs some measures of integrity and self-respect, and prestige if possible. The objects are the same; it is how he responds to them that marks out his peculiarities.

The individual is a bundle of needs; most of his actions are taken on their behalf, for while they are unsatisfied they are painful. The body is equipped with special nerve fibers which act as receptors of pain which can be sharp or mere discomforts; in any case they are signs that something is missing. When an organ is deprived of something it needs, it sends signals through the brain centers to the muscles. All such signals from one nerve cell to another are of the same size, like the dots without the dashes of the Morse code, the intensity of the signals being made up of their frequency. By means of this language the muscles are instructed to work the skeleton. The individual acts in this way to obtain the necessary materials from his environment. Usually he has to transform them; food is cooked, water purified, shelters constructed. Thus objects of culture are brought into existence by the kind of behavior described as "aggression" because it always involves a certain amount of force.

No individual occupies the environment alone, each one has to engage in cooperation or competition for its goods, also a form of aggression, whether it is between members of the human species or between species (predator-prey interactions). With the latter, there is destruction as well as construction; the destruction of other animals, say, and the promotion of the welfare of the human animal. When aggression takes a constructive form the interaction between the individual and his environment produces changes in his nervous system (learning) as well as changes in the environment (artifacts).

The word "artifacts" is now a description of almost everything in the surroundings of civilized man, from streets to books, from buildings to violins — any material thing which he has made over.

The individual who lives in such surroundings continues to feel the deprivation of organic needs. This is the "single-drive theory," and a serious objection has been raised to it on the grounds that such needs are still felt when the organs they represent are absent. Hunger is felt by patients whose stomachs have been surgically removed, and thirst has remained when the throat has been anesthetized.

The answer to this objection may be that the needs are centered in organs early in life but not confined there. Motivation involves the activity of the whole organism. As the young individual develops, the need spreads throughout his whole body; and while organs continue to be the agents of organisms, it is the whole body that has the need.

The Needs in General

The needs of the body fall into a number of well-defined groups, according to where the materials to satisfy them are found. There are those that can be located internally; those that can be obtained on the outside with little effort; and finally those that can be had only by working for them. Let us consider each of these briefly:

The self-operating mechanisms within the body are concerned with internal organization and perform their necessary functions without the assistance or the knowledge of the individual: a regular heart beat, a constant body temperature, growth. The body has an internal environment which must be kept constant. Breathing, sweating and shivering are regulatory processes which accomplish this without deliberate exertion.

There are material things the body needs which are freely available in the environment: air to breathe, land to stand on, gravity to hold the body on the earth, the day-night cycle (recently named the circadian rhythm), and sleep.

These are needs which are naturally-occurring; and because they call on us for nothing extra, though they are crucial to man's existence, nothing more need be said about them here.

What I will talk about at some length is the third set of needs which do require material things from the environment and for which deliberate efforts have to be made. I list three familiar ones and three others which may not be so familiar.

Among the obvious needs are those for water, food and sex. Each is a requirement of some special organ of the body: water for the kidneys, food for the stomach, sex for the gonads. Obtaining them calls on special drives and results in standard interchanges between the body and its environment.

Information, security, and activity are less familiar. To obtain these there exist also special organs and drives: the brain for information, the skin for security, the muscles for activity. I shall have to say a lot more about them, particularly about security, because the role the skin plays here comes as a surprise to many.

The six needs I have mentioned are not as separated as my list would indicate. Curiosity is certainly involved in all six: it requires a certain amount of curiosity to discover where water and food are to come from and to plan how they can be obtained, and it takes a certain amount of activity to obtain them.

There is security in knowing that water and food will continue to be available. I separate the two groups, to emphasize the place each occupies preeminently in the life of the individual.

There are many artificial needs which have been induced in the individual. Addictions belong to this class, the "habit" of using caffeine, nicotine, alcohol or morphine. After repeated uses a need is acquired, resulting in a dependence.

The way the needs make themselves known is through the feelings, which can be pleasurable as well as painful; their satisfactions are pleasurable.

It is with the needs that come from the outside, that I shall be mainly concerned. The sense organs: eyes, ears, mouth, nose, skin, receive the impact of impressions from material things in the external world; a certain amount of thought goes into solving the problem of what to do about those material things and the muscles make the chosen efforts. Just as there is an internal balance which maintains the equilibrium of the organism, so there is an external balance between the organism and its environment.

Consciousness depends on that balance. The individual does not remain conscious unless there is something to be conscious *of*, some novelty mixed in with his experience. This is an astonishing fact, but it is true that when everything in the individual's environment is constant he falls asleep. That is why solitary drivers on straight roads at night and often by day doze at the wheel. Novelty is not only refreshing, it is necessary.

Chief among the organs of sense are the eyes, which provide colored impressions of material things and give some indication of their relative size and location. Patterns are discovered in the perceived object. Yet no individual relies only on his sight. All the senses assist by functioning as guides. The movement of his body will take him up to the object and around it so that he can touch it. If it makes any noise, he can hear it from some distance, and when he gets closer he can smell it. The drives compel him to act as a whole though usually through the agency of his parts.

To some extent he directs his body toward desired goals. Here again the organs perform a service. The brain, for example may be regarded as a distance receptor. It functions in that way through thought, which may be about absent objects; and imagination, which probes into how things are in other worlds.

The individual operates in many arenas, and often on the basis of instinct, which may be described as a kind of built-in adjustment made over many generations to a given environment. It is important to talk about the entire man, his successes and defeats.

To say that an individual is living means that he is continually engaged in efforts of various sorts. As long as there is life in his body he is active. Though some of the activity is mechanical and thoughtless, not all of it is. Most is the result of deliberate, conscious choices. The individual is usually able to select the actions he wants to take. When we say that a course of action was taken without any thought we mean it was determined by previous habits of thought.

Consider how the six needs operate through feeling: the lack of water felt as thirst, the lack of food as hunger, the lack of sex as desire, the lack of information as curiosity, the lack of activity as stiffness, the lack of security as fear. The first three are concerned with immediate survival, the effort to stay alive, the survival of what I will henceforth call the short-range self, while the last three are occupied with ultimate survival, with immortality and the long-range self. We will take a closer look at them in the following two chapters.

Chapter IV
Immediate Survival and the Short-Range Self

Importunate versus Important Needs

There is an important distinction between importunate needs —
the most urgent ones — and important needs which may be
pursued more slowly but have considerably greater consequences. In the light of this distinction I divide the needs into
those concerned with immediate survival, with what I call the
short-range self — needs for water, food and sex — and those
concerned with ultimate survival and the long-range self —
curiosity, security and activity. Of course everyone has all the
needs in some measure, though they differ widely in different
people. Some never get past the basics for one reason or another;
those who manage to continue their drives into the territory laid
out for the important needs make the environment for the others
as well as for themselves.

Let us look then first at the three most basic needs: for water,
for food and for sex.

Thirst — and What Follows from It

The need for water is considered the most pressing. Water is the most abundant chemical in the body and also in the diet. A man who weighs 150 pounds contains about seven gallons of water (women tend to be fatter and so need slightly less). A man would be dead if he lost water to the extent of 15 per cent of his body weight.

Thus when five pints of water are lost in a day of light work indoors, and twenty pints during heavy work in the sun, they must be replaced on a daily basis. Given water and no food a man can survive for several months, but without water for only ten days.

The need for food is not felt after a few days but thirst never stops. Desert people naturally know more about the importance of water than anyone else. Their idea of heaven is a place with abundant fountains flowing with fresh water.

Water is to be found everywhere in the body. It acts as a solvent, it is a cooling agent in the form of perspiration, and it helps to oxidize food and eliminate waste; its deprivation is felt most strongly in the throat. It is of special importance to the kidneys, dry kidney tissue deteriorates very quickly without water. The chief task of the kidneys is the removal of waste products, which would not be possible without a fresh supply of water.

We seldom remember how much our existence depends upon simple things. Water is a common everyday substance — hardly a stimulating one, noted chiefly when absent — clear, transparent, in thick layers colored bluish-green, halfway in solidity between air and crystal, inconsequential-seeming — yet life-giving. Water, like so much in plentiful supply, seems trivial. Yet everything depends on it and great social provision is made for it, but after that it is taken for granted unless the supply fails us. It is usually so highly available that it requires no special attention. This was not true in California in the winter of 1977, when there was a drouth, felt very keenly in Marin County, and special efforts had to be made also in some other counties to preserve it.

Hunger — and Its Consequences

To say that food is a need of the stomach is to press the case a little; I should have said of the entire digestive and assimilation system of the alimentary canal, which begins when food enters the mouth and passes down the throat to the duodenum before reaching the stomach and moving on into the intestine.

Food takes about four hours to move through the stomach, which has a capacity of 2½ pints and is primarily a container for storing and mixing. Its walls secrete digestive juices, chiefly hydrochloric acid, but it does not absorb very much. Most digestion and the absorption of food takes place through the walls of the intestines which run some 28 feet from the stomach to the anus. At the end of the digestive process is the liver, which receives through the portal vein all the materials that have been absorbed by the intestines. Because its various functions have been counted in the hundreds, it has been called a chemical factory, the central organism of metabolism responsible for those energy exchanges which mark the end of the food process.

No one will be much disposed to argue against the importance of hunger as a need. When it is frustrated the consequent drive tends to obscure all other needs. Cannibalism is one of the oldest of human practices and probably long predates the species. Despite the abhorrence in which it is held today, circumstances are always capable of provoking its practice. There is an account of one such occurrence as recently as 1974 among the survivors of a plane wreck in the Andes.

Joe E. Lewis the comedian once remarked that "Thanks to the benefits of modern medicine, the sick native of today is the healthy head-hunter of tomorrow." The hunger drive overcomes all reluctance, as isolated occurrences of cannibalism occasionally testify. Someone has remarked that for any of us it is never more than sixteen meals away.

Sexual Desire – and its Results

The third of the primary needs is for sex, and it is of course a need of the gonads and ovaries, in some way connected with the limbic system of the brain. Other parts of the brain may be even more intimately involved, however.

It is well established that there is a pleasure center in the brain which can be stimulated when electrodes are implanted in the hypothalamus or the amygdala, and indications are that the feeling is sexual. Human subjects treated in this way report pleasurable feelings in the pelvic region.

Unlike the other primary needs sex is social, usually (though not always) requiring a partner. For the male it is the need to expel semen, for the female to receive it. Both involve physiological processes that are pleasurable in a way not too well understood.

The periodicity of sexual activity varies greatly, from several times a day to once a month or so, the average being about twice a week. In the life of the individual it plays a considerable role.

The needs themselves are only raw materials; it is how men shape the drives to reduce the needs that counts. Sexual activity can be aggressively or altruistically conducted, according as it is dedicated to selfish pleasure or to that of a partner.

The sex drive is also a reproductive drive, a secondary one in the case of men but usually, if not always, a primary one for women. In most women the maternal instinct is very strong and extends well beyond the activities of conception and birth. Indeed its longest phase only begins at birth, for children have to be protected and cared for through all the years of their helplessness.

One consequence is that inside every thin girl there is a thick mother struggling to get out, a result of love-making that most men carefully avoid thinking about at the time (which may perhaps be taken to mean that love by itself is not a good reason for doing anything).

Anticipating and Planning

Man, unlike many other animals, can foresee that his needs will be pressing on him in the days to come in much the same way that they have in the past. Other living organisms do share this anticipation and endeavor to provide for it, but no other animal extends it to successive generations, none tries for instance to insure a supply of water and food for its descendants.

Man constructs water systems, conduits and plumbing city-wide; he makes reservoirs and arranges for water to be pumped to where it is needed. He builds farms and ranches; most of the land in any country is under cultivation if it is fertile land. Farming and stock raising are bedrock activities in any society. These are not activities for the solitary individual. No man ever built an entire water system by himself; few have made a farm or stocked a ranch alone.

Every one of the individual's activities in search of need reductions leads him into some degree of cooperation with his fellows, thus contributing to the establishment of society.

The social nature of these three basic needs is best exemplified by hunger. Farming is rarely the work of a single individual; but farming communities are common. The pursuit of food is a social undertaking, but accounts in history of crop failures are not infrequent. The joint effort to obtain sufficient food is probably the most social of all, and therefore the *sine qua non* of civilization.

Chapter V
Ultimate Survival and the Long-Range Self

Curiosity— and what it leads to

Information is a tissue need of the brain, an immensely complex organ containing an estimated 9 billion nerve cells but operating on an electric current of only 25 watts. One authority questions whether new branches of mathematics will not have to be discovered before anyone is in a position to understand its complexities.

The mind is connected with the brain through the body's nervous activity in some way not well understood. Attempts to reduce the mind to the brain have not been entirely successful; yet where there is no brain, there can be no mind. Mental states can be controlled by modifications of the brain, and so it must be the brain and not the mind which is the operative center even though the mind plays an important role.

The word "mind" is commonly used to include consciousness in its various states of alertness, also the unconscious (memory) and the control of behavior. The mind is the way in which the individual is aware of what is happening to him, it sits in judgment

47

on what comes before him, and decides on actions, which he sometimes can and sometimes cannot carry out.

It might be described as the government of the country of the individual, which is a loose democracy with only a limited amount of control exercised over the organs of the body.

We know some important facts about the mental life. Unless the mind receives a certain amount of information in childhood it will not develop, and much of this lack cannot be made up later. Hence the importance of education. The information, of course, comes from that external world with which the individual makes contact through his sense organs and muscles.

I use the term "information" rather than "knowledge" for a particular reason; I do mean knowledge but I mean also the degree of order, for this is the way the word is used in theories of communication.

Memory seems to be composed of the many "bits" of information made possible by modifying some elements of cells in the brain, resulting in permanent changes. The information contained in the brain is carried by molecules, called polyneucleotides, and is arranged by it in a special way in chains of pairs.

The enormous complexity and the size of this system has to be studied to be believed. The brain as an information storage facility may be the most complex thing known. There is built into it an inherited capacity for learning and using language. Millions of years of evolution were required to reach this point in the development of the species. Thus no one language is innate but the ability to learn a language is.

Communication between individuals by means of speech seems also to be provided for. It has been located in the brain, but in one area chiefly, the left hemisphere, where there is an enlargement not matched on the other side. Stimulation of the right hemisphere produces calls and cries but not expressive language. Infants are evidently born with this asymmetry.

Every experience lays down new memories. It is on the basis of previous experiences that decisions are made respecting courses of action. This exercise of choice is called the will. The will operates also on the memory. It interprets the past by selecting. There is a wonderful illustration of this in Chekhov's play *The Three Sisters*.

In one scene an elderly daughter is talking to her widowed father. "Were you in love with mother?" she asks. "Yes," he replies after some hesitation, "yes, I was." "And was she in love with you?" He shakes his head sadly, "I can't remember."

The possession of information serves the individual in two ways: it helps him to know where and in what manner he can reduce his immediate needs, and it helps him to reduce his ultimate needs as well. We do not know how decisions respecting actions are made but we do know that they involve choosing between alternative courses.

The ignorant are not lacking in knowledge, what they are lacking is *true* knowledge. They have an immense amount of false knowledge, which is always simpler than true and easier to maintain, and any effort to remove it encounters immense inertia. Much of life is conducted on the basis of erroneous information; unfortunately, nothing is so disastrous to successful practice as the faithful application of a false theory.

The false application of a true theory also can be disastrous. There is a good illustration in the film *The Bridge On The River Kwai,* made in 1968. In the second world war, so the story goes, some American prisoners of the Japanese were put to work in the jungle building a railroad bridge for the enemy. Now obviously the better they performed their task, the worse for the American cause, since the bridge was intended to be used to facilitate Japanese troop movements. But the American officer the Japanese had put in charge was a conscientious man accustomed to seeing that things were done right. His fellow prisoners who were working on the job could not make him recognize, until disaster struck at the very end of their efforts, that efficiency in this case had the opposite effect of the one intended and that success from the American point of view spelled failure.

The central activity of the brain is thought, believed to be connected with the frontal lobes. Thought may consist in signals which come in through the senses and then get involved in some sort of holding process of closed pathways in the nervous system.

The brain not only works over the data that comes to it but itself acts as a distance receptor, connecting things close by with those remote in space and time and so out of reach of the senses. Thought, in other words, links up present things with absent things through a general language invented to cover both.

Thinking may be regarded as a complex form of bodily behavior, not too unlike other bodily skills which it resembles and from which it may have developed. The activity of thought is aided by the device of language which furnishes the means of communicating and recording information. Language begins with signs having meaning. Words are signs that refer to things, so language engages in reference. It is sometimes forgotten that the references of language lie outside language in those objects to which the language refers. Only the meanings stay inside the language.

There are two kinds of objects referred to in language: material things and abstract things. The material things are easy to understand and recognize, such things as the earth, William Shakespeare, the city of London, things that are unique and can therefore be easily named. The abstract things present a little more difficulty: words that name classes of things, such as chairs, circles and pairs. It will be noticed at once that there are differences here in the inclusiveness of the references: "chairs" names all the material objects of a certain kind that exist in the universe. "Circles" has a larger reference, for it names all round things, including round chairs. The reference of "pairs" is still larger, the largest of all, for it names two of anything, including two chairs and two circles.

The names of classes of material things do not name *material* things, only their *classes*. We must have another word for them, and we do: we call them "universals" because what they name is the same wherever — and whenever — it occurs throughout the universe, a *universal name* for a *universal thing*.

It is seldom recognized that the language we use ordinarily

consists chiefly in universals, which are after all nothing more than general ideas. In the sentence "Give me a cigarette" every word is a universal. Although readers are not usually aware of it, most of the words in the dictionary are universals. The exceptions are what we have talked about already, proper names, the names of material things, of particulars, rare enough in dictionaries though occurring frequently in common speech.

Thus all words are names. Most words name classes and so are called universals, some words name material things and so are called particulars. In the formation of sentences the words connecting the names are themselves universal names. All verbs are universals, and so are all the other parts of speech.

Practical knowledge uses sentences to tell us something universal about a particular. For example, "Lincoln had a strong character and was an influential leader." Theoretical knowledge employs sentences connecting many universals. The laws of the physical sciences and all of pure mathematics are of this latter type. They tell us something very valuable because they describe events that always happen in the same way, and thus provide us with some measure of control over the future. All animals exhibit purposive behavior, but in man it has a much more extended range.

Every discovery in the sciences opens up new areas, but, unfortunately, as knowledge increases so does ignorance. No one for example understands the nature of those short-range forces which hold the constituents of the atom together, but it is not many decades since we first found out about this valuable lack of knowledge. To know what we do not know leads to further inquiry. Wonder keeps pace with information.

It is fortunate that the individual can make the decisions necessary to produce a society, for he can survive only as a member of it. Yet every idea that was ever carried out in social life issued first from the brain of a single individual. If societies are to survive and grow, the individual's unique capacity to think about problems in order to initiate concerted actions must be preserved. How to maintain the balance between individual freedom and social organization is therefore one of the most pressing problems of our time.

Security— and Its Far-Ranging Consequences

The need of the individual to continue his existence is strong. As Sir Thomas Browne wrote in 1685, "the long habit of living indisposeth us for dying". Men do live longer than most other animals but usually they survive to little more than 70 years. The oldest recorded ages considered authentic are those of individuals who lived some 115 years. Only the tortoise manages a few more. But man, unlike the other animals, knows that he must die, and so he looks for ways of continuing his existence.

Security means freedom from danger; safety. When I say that security is a tissue need of the skin, I know the statement takes a good deal of explaining; I think the evidence points strongly in that direction.

The skin as an organ is the essence of uniqueness: The skin of one individual does not accept a permanent graft from the skin of another but only from another part of the body of the same individual. It is also one of the largest organs of the human body, and provides a covering which must be penetrated before the organism can be injured. It is in a sense the first line of defense.

The drive for security takes two forms. The first is to work for the continuance of existence by protecting and extending the finite life of the body (the short-range self). The second is to prevent the end of existence from ever happening, and this is an activity in favor of the finite life of the long-range self beyond the life of the body.

It is because of his skin that man seeks shelter and protective clothing when the weather brings too much warmth from the sun's heat or too much cold from snow and ice. The skin makes immediate and direct contact with the things in the near environment, reporting back to the senses what it has encountered, responding in compulsory movements of approach and avoidance in an environment containing both safety and danger. For the short-range self the skin signals threats as well as friendliness and can be watched closely for indications of either. Thus it affects behavior in an immediate way.

Immediate security, then, is an affair of the contact of the skin with near-by objects offering safety to the short-range self. But what about the long-range self? What about ultimate security?

Sexual intercourse of course involves skin contact; another kind of activity taken by the individual in his search for ultimate security is one that requires no special effort on his part: reproduction. Children are by-products of the sexual drive though often sought as ends in themselves. Long-range security is provided for most individuals through the preservation of the species.

The desire to live forever seems particularly human. The individual can always look ahead and see that his life will end, and so he makes frantic efforts to avoid it. This need amounts to a deep craving, and takes the odd form of responding to the quality of those material objects which represent permanence. Here again the skin plays an important part.

To satisfy all his needs an individual would have to control all of his environment. Since this is manifestly impossible as a goal of action, he has turned to the use of symbols. His skin has become an agent of contact with objects in the far distance, though only in a symbolic way.

Here mysticism, and even magic, enter the picture, for the symbols the skin is in contact with are those used in religious ceremonials; sacred symbols representing the most powerful and farthest removed of objects: the universe or its cause. In primitive tribes imitative magic operates through such symbolic contact, and in the religions of civilization this primitive practice is still present. A good example is to be found in the sacraments of the Roman Catholic Church, all involving touch of some sort, from the wafer and wine of the Eucharist to the ritual of Extreme Unction. For Moslems there is the kissing of the black stone at Mecca and for Hindus the image of the Buddha.

There are other approaches to ulimately security, however.

Consider the contributions of those originative individuals who produce works of art, make discoveries in the sciences, or put together systems of philosophy which function as security systems because absolute belief provides a feeling of safety. A philosophy is seldom presented as what it is, and is usually unconsciously assumed as a faith by those belonging to a church, or as a set of principles by the citizens of a state; it can be found imbedded in the formal beliefs of a religion, for instance, or those of a political party. The philosophical content, considered as theology or political theory, satisfies the deep need of the individual for an absolute truth, something that he is sure will never let him down and that appeals strongly to his emotionally-held convictions.

The security of the long-range self lies finally in living within an institution which seems more inclusive than any other. This is the outcome of man's craving for a continuance of his existence because it promises him immortality either through the salvation of his soul or by means of some share in the future of works in this world.

The discussion of ultimate security compels us to look at the life of the spirit. I used the word "spirit" with some hesitation because over the centuries it has meant so many different things, and to use it now in a precise way involves some risk of being misunderstood.

"By "spirit," then, I mean here not the time-honored notion of an animating principle or soul capable of surviving the body but rather the dominant inner quality of any material thing, a property of all matter. The higher and more complex a material thing is, the more important the role played in it by the spirit, and because the most complex thing known is the human brain with its nine billion inter-connected nerve cells, when we think of spirit it is chiefly the human spirit that we mean, a response to the quality of the universe.

Man is highest in the scale of material things. His body is the most organized and most complex of all such things, and therefore spirit plays a very significant role in his feelings and consequently also in his thoughts and actions. Spirit requires the loftiest sort of feeling, a feeling of harmony with the universe; though not always conscious, it is connected with consciousness. It is what guides the individual in his most comprehensive expressions. We recognize the spirit in man because it is in man alone that it has risen to such a peak of intensity. The individual encounters the spirit within himself as his self-consciousness; others are able to judge it from the outside by his behavior.

The spiritual life is the life of the individual in so far as he seeks that same spirit in others and in the whole of the universe. The dominant inner quality of the material universe as a whole can be felt by concentrating on its two most characteristic features: its immensity and its permanence. Hence the strenuous and elaborate efforts made by individuals to identify with it.

Activity— what it does, and undoes

The muscles do most of the work in the human body, from operating the heart to moving the bones. To say that activity is a tissue need of the muscles, therefore, is to state the most obvious fact. Every muscle works through the all-or-nothing principle: it contracts or it does not. The movements of the body are the work of the muscles but only by pulling, they are not capable of pushing. When an individual pushes against something he is utilizing energy converted from muscles pulling. There are 656 muscles altogether, more than three times as many as bones. If the muscles are unused even for a short length of time they atrophy; a broken arm wrapped in a cast for some weeks shows marked deterioration.

The individual is always engaged in muscular activities of some sort even if they are only internal: the beating of the heart, the flow of blood through the blood vessels, involuntary stretch or contraction. Even in sleep the internal movements continue, and there is an occasional shifting of the body. Of course aimless movements do exist, as when one is restless, but most activity is aimed: there is always a movement in search of some external goal because if life is to be maintained the energy expended must be replaced.

Man acts in most instances on the basis of feelings rather than reasons. The feelings of a rational individual are more reasonable than those of an irrational one, which is the chief justification for reasoning. Since feelings lead to actions, reasoning must take place in advance of the feelings. Once the individual finds himself in a crisis situation, it is usually too late to weigh alternatives or anticipate possible consequences, too late, in a word, to think. Decisions have to be made concerning actions in the heat of the actions, which for a waking individual never stop.

So unceasing is the demand of the musculature for activity that it often becomes an end in itself: action for the sole sake of action. The popularity of violent sports attests to this claim; even the threat of physical danger is not a deterrent.

There was no lack of gladiators in ancient Rome or of men to joust in the Middle Ages. The Mayans of Central America and southern Mexico played a version of basketball in which the captain of the losing team had his heart cut out. Dangerous games still exist.

It may be true, as the English thinker Hobbes said, that life is "nasty, brutish and short," but it is also true that it is exciting, and for this men will take all sorts of risks. Mountain climbing and deep sea diving exact their toll. Even in football or hockey injuries are common.

Primitive man did not need to make special arrangements in order to get enough exercise, as civilized man does. Life in cities does not usually involve the strenuous use of muscles, so football fields, basketball courts, gymnasiums and tennis courts have been built. But somehow the sedentary life reasserts itself and instead of exercising it becomes the habit of most people to watch professional athletes exercising; a curious substitution.

Judging by the number of people involved and the amounts paid to athletes, professional sports are big business. They provide the kind of vicarious experience of aggression which seems to be necessary because of the sedentary nature of modern life. The excitement generated by the spectators of sporting events is unproductive; nothing follows from it. Unlike the emotions produced by the appreciation of the arts, spectator sports tend to leave the observer emptier and more letdown than he was before.

Man is preeminently the maker, happy when dedication to some constructive activity takes him out of himself and he is able to think only about what he is striving to accomplish. In the use of the muscles, however, destruction is more efficient; there is a very pleasurable type of need reduction to be found in raw, overt aggression. It issues in the effort to dominate the environment in order to reduce all the needs together, the aim of the ambitious man of action, whether he be politician or industrialist. Such domination involves intimidation, coercion and the use of force generally. The needs of the muscles are geared to violence, and are not to be satisfied by peaceful movements except temporarily.

Because of his need for food, man lives by killing other animals and plants, but unfortunately killing in order to live may lead easily to living in order to kill. We have successfully deceived ourselves from time to time about what constitutes our essential humanity by remembering only the favorable features: the gentleness, the humility, the sympathy, and by overlooking the brutality, the sadism, the ferocity. Yet no one can hope to understand human nature without recognizing the extremes of exaggerated behavior of which we are capable: ultimate self-sacrifice, but also, and more commonly, unbelievable cruelty, which, though it has been recognized for some time, is often forgotten. In European museums instruments invented in the Middle Ages for the specific purpose of torture may still be seen. Those in wide use today in many civilized countries are simply not on view. It is interesting in this connection that in the ancient Persian religion Zoroaster recognizes the existence of twin Spirits; in addition to a Holy Spirit there was also a Destructive Spirit which "chooses to do the worst things." The Nazi holocaust is not so far behind us; the Nazis killed some 16 million people in cold blood. In 1976 the Cambodian communists murdered over a million of their countrymen. In Africa, as in Asia, genocide is common. The massacres of Acholi and Lango tribesmen in Uganda in 1977 were matched by the earlier massacre of Ibos in Nigeria and by the 200,000 Hutus killed in Burundi in the 1960s.

In every society there are doubtless all sorts of conflicting tendencies among social groups, sadism in some and altruism in others. The kind of man found in the secret police who enjoys inflicting pain on the political prisoners who fall into his hands, and the kind of man who volunteers for charitable social work to help the underprivileged, are always present but not equally prominent.

Which group rises to power and exercises its prerogative is often a result of many causes; nothing in any organization as complex as a society is ever singly caused. Thus torture or philanthropy may be the prevailing custom according to the results of the forces at work. Violent activity seems to be a periodic need, hence the prevalence of wars. In his *Anabasis* the Greek soldier-historian Xenophon, in telling the story of the Persian expedition against Athens, wrote that "one of the results of power is to take what belongs to the weaker." In our own day the Soviet Union seized the Baltic states and maintains garrisons in Hungary and Czechslovakia, while Communist China invaded and occupied Tibet.

Peace is a result of the temporary equilibrium between forces of love and hate; when that equilibrium is upset, social changes occur. And so there is a continuing ambivalence of aggression: strenuous efforts made by man to help his fellow men and equally strenuous efforts to hurt them. Evidently the conflicting drives of the muscles which impel people toward both the arts of peace and the spoils of war are equally powerful. Sometimes the two drives occur together. During the Renaissance the Borgias ruled in Italy for thirty years over a period of warfare, terror and murder, in the kind of bloodbath seldom witnessed; that same period also produced Michelangelo, Leonard da Vinci, and many other genuises. Sometimes long stretches of peace as in Switzerland have produced little that is constructive.

Chapter VI
The Needs in General

The range of human behavior — what paradoxically might be described as the extremes of human behavior in the normal range — has always been underestimated. The style of behavior is often an index to its meanings. Style — style in the grand sense — is economy of activity raised to the level of art.

In contrast, there are the innumerable examples of contemporary foolishness, the man who suffers from the heat by keeping the windows closed in his car during the summer because he wants his neighbors to think that he can afford air conditioning, the people who in 1976 were paying money for "pet rocks," buying kitchen gadgets that make square eggs, talking to plants.

All the Needs Together

The life of the individual is an indivisible whole, not an affair of separate needs. Let us consider how the six organic drives work together, as they must, to operate successfully. Because the individual acts with his whole body, he can drive to meet only one need at a time. He must therefore establish a system of priorities if he hopes to give to each of his needs the attention it requires.

But even when the needs are assigned an order, they compete, each seeking to gain more than its share of the total effort. The priorities vary to some extent from individual to individual, but in general it may be said that the primary needs are the more pressing, the secondary needs the more important: the primary are the means *by* which, the secondary the ends *for* which.

We have already noted that the first group serves the short-range self, the individual in his immediate need to survive, and that the second group serves the long-range self, the individual in his ultimate need to exist forever. The minute the former is taken care of temporarily — it is never more than that — the latter presses its claims.

There are times when sex seems more important than happiness and other times when the individual asks himself whether he has the moral right to enjoy himself even in socially acceptable ways. No wonder that there is often a conflict between the drives for short-range and for long-range survival.

The politician and the businessman are less concerned with their ultimate fate than the poet and painter who do not pay sufficient attention to food and rent. Each may seem somewhat foolish to the other, but it is to the politicians and businessmen that their contemporaries tend to listen.

It is not uncommon for two needs to cooperate in a single drive. Curiosity often leads the individual into exploratory behavior, the activity of manipulating the environment, or of traveling to new places. Play, which is usually work done from the simple need to expend energy, is often to be found in combination with aggression in competitive games requiring an outcome in the proven superiority of victory. It is also not uncommon for one drive to trigger another in a way which lies outside the individual's control. Fear may provoke anger. Sexual arousal may lead to unprovoked aggression; and conversely aggression may lead to sexual arousal.

It is advisable to distrust strong feelings until they have been certified by reason, and to examine carefully all rational arguments when they provoke strong feelings.

We noted at the outset that each of the organs is an agent acting on behalf of the organism, which benefits as a whole from the satisfaction of a particular need. Yet there is no doubt that individual needs conflict, and driving to reduce one need may inhibit drives to reduce others. They cannot all be reduced at the same time, and one drive sometimes cuts across others. Individuals have been known to renounce all sexual activity because they believed it was required of them by some religious faith.

In general it is true that no individual worries about his immortality when he is hungry. Once that need is taken care of, a deeper sense of insecurity returns. People are often "helpless with laughter" or "paralyzed by fear." Curiosity and fear, the fear of what is strange, for example, may tend to offset each other, as they do in the well known dual reaction of approach and avoidance; the impulse to draw near to a strange object and the equally strong impulse to avoid it, leading to a point halfway between the two drives where they balance. The task of reducing all of the needs is never finished. The chief purpose of the individual consists in his efforts to see this task accomplished. What would it mean, we may ask, to have all of the needs satisfied, what would be the result?

The feeling of well-being consists in the efficient functioning of the whole individual in all his properly coordinated parts. But this is only a goal for striving, not the recognition of an achievement.

To be successful in reaching perfection in terms of the environing world would mean that the muscles would have overcome all resistance; the skin would have made contact with the entire universe (or its cause); knowledge would have been completed. The world would have been assimilated to the individual, while for him perfection would be more like death.

There is in every individual a core of irrationality, perhaps resulting from conflicting drives which have effects he does not anticipate. Recognized generally as "the imp of the perverse" it is the impulse that at some point makes every individual his own worst enemy. It either defeats a rational program at its start or leads an individual to carry one out even when he can foresee that it will be a failure.

There are other difficulties common enough to be familiar. When a doctrine makes a great appeal yet goes against human nature, it is retained all the same after being adjusted to fit. The doctrine of Christian love was established within a framework which included "justifiable wars" of religion.

It is so with many drives. For instance, the drive for sexual satisfaction may continue long after the sexual need has been reduced, becoming more like the drive to dominate the environment in its Don Juan phase of collecting conquests. Any drive may occupy the individual's entire energy, and so become the sole reason for his existence, thus inhibiting all other drives. This blocking effect produces the exaggerated actions which the ancient Greeks recognized so clearly as "outrageous behavior," but it produces also the selfless devotion to causes, and it produces monuments of art, religion and science. Outrageous behavior fits well with man's strong appetites which exceed those of any other animal. It is worth underscoring that *in every one of his efforts at need reduction he endeavors to exceed himself.* In man, unlike the other animals, a drive does not stop when a need is reduced. The response made to the need always exceeds the stimulus provided by the material objects which promise need reduction.

Thus he arranges to tap more water than he can ever drink, to store more food than he can ever eat, to collect more women than he can ever love, to accumulate greater wealth than he can ever spend. As to his secondary needs, he recognizes that nothing less than the conquest and domination of his entire environment will ever be sufficient.

Hunting appeals very much to men because it would be difficult to go to war and still be back in time for work on Monday. For a holy war, though, almost anyone would be willing to take the time off.

Man wants to be more than man, that is the essence of what it means to be human, an arrow aimed at eternity.

He has the ambition if not the potentiality for the unlimited aggression necessary to subdue the universe. He would be god if he could. But he must settle for less, and if he has to reconcile himself with others who have the same ambition, that is not calculated to add to his happiness.

Emotions as Frustrated Needs

The drives intended to reduce the needs do not always succeed in reaching their goal objects. Some of those that do not succeed end by producing emotions. Much of the emotional life is connected with the frustration of some strong need, some organic drive which has not been carried out in action. Emotion is the response of the whole organism to the blocking of behavior. Impulses which ordinarily would lead to activities are instead referred to the central nervous system. There presumably impulses occur which are discharged in feeling.

Any organ deprivation may be the occasion for an expression of emotion.

Perhaps the most common is fear, which arises from a threat to continued existence.

Rage is the outcome of actions of a violent nature which had been expected by the muscles but not carried out; anger is the result of withheld action.

Hate and hostility result from fixing on a particular object as the cause of the frustration.

Sexual passion is an emotion felt as frustration until dissipated by intercourse. Monotonous repetition tends to reduce the capacity of an object to satisfy a need. In the words of the behaviorists, it is negatively reinforcing. Marriage has been wryly described as combining a maximum of opportunity with a minimum of temptation.

Grief is the frustration at loss, deprivation and shock, followed by reconciliation.

Laughter, which involves a peculiar reaction of excitement, a breathing disturbance and series of short noises, comes from recognizing the extent to which things-as-they-are fall short of things-as-they-ought-to-be. Both grief and laughter are in their separate ways expressions of frustration at situations which cannot be prevented.

Hope is a postponed identification with an object promising security for the long-range self.

Ambition represents the somewhat frantic and excessive demand for such identification, foreseen but as yet unobtained.

The emotions common to art and religion are both expressions of empathy; the recognition of far-flung connections are always accompanied by strong emotions.

The aesthetic emotion is the pleasure which accompanies the deliberate apprehension of beauty in a material object, with beauty understood as the quality which emerges from the relation of parts in a whole. For the individual it means a sort of superfluous caring, in which he has no desire to change the world, only to love it.

The religious emotion comes about because the "work of art" is the whole universe, and its recognition the feeling of a deep and abiding sense of ultimate belonging. True religious emotion involves dedication, not personal advantage; another variety of superfluous caring, this time for the holy, which carries an equal value for all things.

Chapter VII
The Social Environment

From Individual Needs to Social Institutions

While every one wishes to be treated as though he were unique, most individuals behave like members of large classes. I know a lawyer who lives in a medium-sized city in the United States with his wife and children. I know the social clubs to which he belongs, the kind of law he practices, the kind of life he leads. If I were to point out to him that he is a stereotype, that there are many like him in other towns and cities, far from disturbing his sense of individuality it would only serve to reinforce his feeling of security. He wants to flock into fold.

Man is a social animal, conditioned by those activities in which he participates with his fellows, and powerful responses deep within him have been formed as a result: strong group loyalties and strong group antagonisms.

Social feeling is represented by the satisfaction of engaging in joint enterprises and by the reinforcement derived from social approval. Shared experiences intensify man's reactions and ease the burdens of his labor, there is safety in numbers; the routines of work groups are established for the accomplishments of common tasks and for the mutual protection of persons and property.

The earliest human populations were small; every man worked only for himself and his family, but as the numbers grew and special talents began to emerge, it became obvious that there were many different skills. Thus there arose the practice of specialization: some individuals stitched hides to make clothing for all the members of the social group, others did the hunting. Out of this kind of division social organizations arose that were large enough to contain the specialists.

Here, then, is the origin of social classes and indeed of the whole class system. The earliest classes were probably only three in number: farmers, artisans, and rulers who were also warriors. As the society grew, more were added: traders, healers, priests, many others.

There were classes but no "class struggle." Marx derived his social theory from a supposed class struggle because he lived at a time when the industrial system of manufacture was just beginning and workers were oppressed by the new factory owners. This is not the case any longer.

In the United States and the countries of western Europe the large labor unions have made an enormous difference. As the wages and benefits of laborers represent a large share of the profits of their work, union members understand that unless industry flourishes, owners and workers will suffer equally. Government frequently sides with the unions because of the large block of votes they represent.

Classes have not always struggled against one another, often they have cooperated, their members living in harmony. Each special group requires the functioning of the others; a society is strong to the extent to which its classes do not compete and are not weakened by the struggle for supremacy.

It is customary to identify a man with his class by the work he does, on the assumption that his economic activity is the cause of his other activities. This is very far from being the case.

There is more to the individual than his class affiliation, which may not have been his free choice but only a matter of economic necessity: most individuals in order to earn a living are compelled to work at whatever tasks are available. Rare is the individual who would have selected the job he has. His employment should not be regarded as having been inevitable or calculated to explain adequately everything else in his life. An individual is whatever he is quite apart from what he does to earn a living.

How then does the individual choose the work to which for the most part he will devote his life? He gravitates toward some enterprise perhaps because of his special talents but often merely by chance. Who is to say, then, how the individual comes to identify his interests with those of a particular institution? Life consists in a series of choices, with the crucial ones hidden. Though this presents a challenge to human ingenuity, it is somewhat onesided. We have Shakespeare's word in *Troilus and Cressida* (1, iii, 33-4) that

> In the reproof of chance
> Lies the true proof of men

The world is a jungle of opportunities and obstacles, with the individual compelled to pick his way. Inheritance as much as the accidents of environment may guide the selection.

Classes are not merely economic divisions, they are functional divisions, and as such dependent upon the services which their members perform for the whole of the society.

* * *

To sum up: the process by which individuals acting separately got together and arranged themselves in institutions began with the organic needs of the individual and his drives to satisfy those needs. Groups of individuals having similar needs cooperated by inventing artifacts and by acquiring skills to operate them.

An institution exists because a certain need common to many individuals is recognized as permanent. Since the responses exceed the stimulus, a regular channel for need reductions must be provided. Reducing one set of needs means temporarily frustrating others, and out of this process installations emerge; to contain the stream, banks must be built higher.

There are lines of connection running from the organic needs of the individual to the corresponding social establishment, with individuals and artifacts brought together to serve a single human need.

Think of the organization of men and artifacts it takes to operate a utility system which provides power for a city, an airline, a department of state, a postal service. Being human may be an animal affair, but being social is not. Society is made up as much of tools and instruments as it is of the individuals who use them, and so in order to understand human nature more deeply, we must take a closer look at institutions.

The Make-up of Institutions

How does an institution operate?

First of all it may be defined as that subdivision of society which consists in social groups established by means of a charter together with their customs, laws and artifacts, organized around a central aim or purpose, a collection of individuals who work together toward a common end. The charter is a set of principles and procedures which gives the institution its measure of stability.

All institutions are serviced by special personnel, men and women whose business it is to run the institution and others who do its work. The distinction is one between the managers of a department store and the salesmen, between the staff of a university and the faculty, between the generals of an army and the fighting units.

The larger the institution the more likely it is to be run by committees, a process which has democratic overtones but also frustrates the decision-making process, for original ideas occur only to individuals.

Obviously the older the institution the more firmly established its traditions, but also the more out-dated; universities, for example, retain the cap and gown for lecturers and academic processions.

The goal-directed elements of institutions are: a creed to which their individual members subscribe, symbols around which their members rally; and if they have lasted for any length of time a particular *style* of behavior by which their members can be recognized; and finally a central aim which it is their purpose to serve.

By way of illustration let us examine one institution, the military: its personnel consists of officers and men; its equipment barracks, guns, uniforms; its procedures drill, the salute; its traditions of service, loyalty, down to the regimental level; its organization a matter of armies and divisions; its creed embodied in the articles of war; its symbols the country's flag together with regimental flags and emblems; its style its military bearing when under orders; its dogma the Constitution of the country; and finally its aim which is to defend the country.

In addition to the primary aim which may differ from one institution to another, there are two secondary aims which all institutions have in common The first is to survive: whatever their primary aim, institutions tend to persist. The second is to increase in size and power, increasing in this way the wealth and prestige of their members.

One illustration will serve to illuminate both the secondary aims.

In 1938, at President Franklin D. Roosevelt's suggestion, an organization to fight poliomyelitis from which he himself had suffered was incorporated as the National Foundation for Infantile Paralysis. (Eddie Cantor first thought of the name by which it was later known, the "March of Dimes.") In 1954 Jonas Salk introduced a vaccine for polio, and in 1960 an oral vaccine developed by Albert Sabin came into wide use. As a result polio practically disappeared. Presumably the work of the foundation called "The March of Dimes" was over, and it would normally have been discontinued, but it was not. The directors chose another ailment, birth defects, and thenceforth devoted the March of Dimes to the new cause.

In 1973 the foundation collected $42.7 million from the public, of which $10 million was saved, $11 million spent in fund raising and overhead, and $22 million devoted to scientific research. The trustees insured Salk's life for $2.4 million with an annual premium of $93,700 because of the asset of his name in fund raising. The March of Dimes still exists, and its savings exceed any need it may have, yet the appeal for funds and their collection continue unabated.

Chapter VIII
The Domain of Institutions

Societies are the domains of institutions. A society may be defined as that organization within a culture whose boundaries are recognized. Institutions are its component parts, and they vary from society to society. A society may be known by the institutions it keeps as well as by how they are ordered.

The Ranking of Institutions

I will divide institutions as I divided needs: into an importunate group serving short-range needs, for water, food and sex, for which the corresponding social institutions to service them were such installations as water purification plants, farms, and the family; and the long-range set of needs, for information, activity and security. Here the corresponding social institutions are many and complex. A list of them organized to promote the satisfaction of curiosity would include schools, libraries, universities and scientific foundations. To promote the satisfaction of activity there are governments and regulated athletic contests. Finally, to promote the satisfaction of the need for security there are religions and the fine arts.

Thus the institutions which become established as a result of the drives to reduce the needs are genuine articles, as necessary to man as his own organs. Social relations embodied in institutions are as solid as anything and must be reckoned with as surely as stones and trees. One who thinks they are not really there learns better when he tries to go against them.

Every individual serves some one institution primarily, but is affected by all institutions, for they interact together in a social whole in which sometimes they are difficult to distinguish. Consider communication, for instance, whose chief medium of exchange is language. Every society has a language which its members speak and write. And it is society-wide, for it affects and is affected by every other institution.

The differences among institutions are made clear by distinguishing four well-defined groups: *constitutive, service, regulative* and *higher* institutions.

The *constitutive* institutions produce the individuals, shape them and provide for them; chiefly the institution of the family but also education and economics.

The *service* institutions help to make the work of other institutions easier; chiefly transportation and communication.

The *regulative* institutions are those which order the society; chiefly the state with its executive (and military), legislative and judicial branches.

The *higher* institutions are those which maintain the aims of the society; chiefly science, art, philosophy and religion. Perhaps the oldest of the higher institutions are art and religion. Because of their peculiar development they merit an extra word. They began as service institutions. The arts were first employed to make signs. Primitive men drew pictures on the walls of caves to indicate the directions in which game could be found. The religions were first engaged in magical invocation of the gods to compel them to assist in promoting the fertility of crops and women. Eventually both institutions became ends in themselves; the fine arts to intensify life, and the religions to preside over its outcome.

No one knows how old art and religion are. Philosophy appeared on the scene only with the classical Greeks some 2600 years ago. Science is the latest arrival; it is no more than five centuries old. Perhaps in the future man will discover and develop others; just now he has to get along with these four.

* * *

Most societies have the same groups of institutions though not always maintaining them in the same order.

> *Constitutive*
> > Family
> > Education
> > Economics
> *Service*
> > Transportation
> > Communication
> *Regulative*
> > State
> > (Executive
> > Legislative
> > Military
> > Judicial)
> *Higher*
> > Science
> > Art
> > Philosophy
> > Religion

Each group contributes something of its own to society. Since the point is such an obvious one, it may be sufficient to sum up the list quickly.

The Constitutive Group. In analyzing society, its organization and artifacts, we must not lose sight of the fact that without people there would be no institution. Man remains fundamental in all of his activities and effects, a product of the basic biological unit: the family.

In connection with this institution there are two others: education and economics: preparing the young for full participation in the society and engaging them in the earning of a living.

The Service Group. These institutions facilitate the work of the others; transportation provides the vehicles to move individuals, communication furnishes the means to exchange meanings and references. The more efficient these service institutions are, the more highly organized, and hence the more advanced, the society.

The Regulative Group. The state is responsible for the order and protection of the society; the executive, legislative and judicial branches to provide order, and the military to offer protection. The effect in any society of the institution of the state is never small, but it is larger in some societies than in others. In some societies the state serves the people; in others the people serve the state.

The Higher Group. The institutions in this group have the common aim of enabling the members of the society to enrich the society. Science has the role of discovering knowledge before technology undertakes to apply it. Art widens and extends what may be called the feeling horizon, while religion softens the effects of living and reconciles man with his destiny.

We will see in chapter IX that the higher group of institutions serves a purpose beyond the narrowly institutional; a cultural purpose.

Conflicts Between Institutions

Men form group loyalties within institutions, loyalties which have side effects in antagonisms between groups, and easily break out in open aggression.

All institutions tend to grow larger, the natural tendency of ambitious individuals operating an institution who want to raise it to first place among institutions. In a certain sense, despite the differences of function, all institutions are competitive. Examples are not difficult to find. Let us glance briefly at a few.

Education versus religion. Education is dedicated to promoting the powers of reasoning. Max Weber pointed out that religions on the other hand have at some stage demanded the sacrifice of reason and a surrender to faith, as when men were exhorted to "believe what is absurd" by Tertullian in the second Christian century. Organized religions are often founded on the insights of prophets with whose statements they are inconsistent. In Buddhism and Christianity wars often followed in the wake of those who preached love.

Business versus the state. A business can become so successful that its size and power threatens the government. The East India Company of English merchants trading in India was granted a charter by Cromwell when it became a joint stock company in 1657. It prospered so greatly thereafter that it began to function as the government of India, thus compelling the English crown in 1858 to take over its administration.

The state versus the fine arts. A conflict exists today in the Soviet Union between politics and literature. The members of the Presidium of the Supreme Soviet take it upon themselves to decide what writings are acceptable even though they lack the qualifications for making such decisions.

The state versus science. Political control of science does not always permit scientific investigation to proceed in the preferred directions. Politicians do not know any more about what problems should be studied in the scientific laboratories than they do about the arts. Thomson, the English physicist, once remarked that if government laboratories had been operating in the Stone Age we would have much improved stone axes but no one would have discovered metals.

The family versus economics. In China for thousands of years the central institution was the family. Many individuals lived in compounds made up of a number of residences. Can we picture reconciling that situation with the multinational companies that operate worldwide today? A family life and worldly business would seem to be incompatible with worldly life and a family business.

The fact remains that in every society institutions must learn how to exist together. To function in harmony (which means in the end to function at all) they must be arranged in some order of importance. Only one, however, can be first. Which one is that to be? The choice differs from society to society, making of each a special case. Societies rarely exist for the primary purpose of transportation or communication. Religion and the military have been more popular choices. Governors exist in order to govern, and sometimes this office, which was designed to be merely facilitative and serviceable, takes over as an end in itself. In the hands of a powerful but unscrupulous ruler this happens easily.

Since all societies have to be regulated, the state is the leading institution in society even though it was designed to exercise only a service function. Who controls the state? Any number of other institutions make the effort. Artists as rulers are rare phenomena, but priests all too frequently have been successful in this role.

Science, a new institution, has moved up the series of institutions very rapidly, and from a comparatively unknown and obscure position now challenges those at the very top. This is certainly true today in both the United States and the Soviet Union; and, given the extraordinary discoveries in the experimental sciences, physics, chemistry and biology, it is likely to be true for some time to come.

In any case it is clear that institutions cannot be left to themselves altogether but must be ranked according to their importance. This is what it means to be a society or a culture: a set of institutions arranged in an order. There is more to it of course, but nearly everything has to be ordered if society is to function in any practical way.

The Leading Institution

Institutions are the chief agencies for the accomplishments of those individuals who are able to triumph over the limitations imposed by the institutions themselves. The institution presents a challenge which only a few individuals meet, those exceptional and powerful originators who eventually turn things around by compelling the institution to adapt to *them*. The institution which benefits most from exceptional behavior on the part of some of its members often becomes the leading institution. In every society one institution dominates the others in important ways, because everything connected with it has a special significance. We can best see what this significance is if we run through it in terms of the eight institutional features.

First the four structural elements:

The *personnel* of the leading institution is usually the highest social class in the society and constitutes its aristocracy: for instance, the scholars in ancient China, the clergy in the Christian Middle Ages, the great landowners in 19th century England, the industrialists in 20th century United States, the members of the Communist Party in the Soviet Union.

Many people do not recognize that there is always an aristocracy though it does not always go by that name. "The rich," declared Tolstoy, "will do anything for the poor except get off their backs." Those who think they can solve this problem by abolishing capitalism need to take a deeper look at Russia. The Communist Party there does not rule with what may be described as a gentle touch. Look at the life of the average citizen in the Soviet Union if you think the government is off his back.

The *equipment* of the leading institution has a special value for the society. I will choose as examples only sacred objects: The thaumaturgic arm of St. Francis Xavier, which was carried about Europe in the second quarter of the 20th century, was not merely an arm; the black stone in Mecca, which all good Moslems kiss, is not merely a piece of stone; the body of Lenin, preserved in a public mausoleum, is not merely a corpse. All have functioned as special symbols.

The *procedures* of the leading institution are the customs which in the society it is most important to follow. Such customs have a native kind of quality, improving the significance felt by its followers, who are thereby made to feel included. Witness the ritual of a church, the routine of a bureaucracy, the discipline of an army.

The *organization* of the leading institution tends to subordinate the others and thus give to the society a much-needed cohesion. Social organization has to be established first from the bottom up;

once established it operates by authority exercised from the top down. So the mother in a traditional matriarchy, the emperor in a divinely-authorized monarchy, the high priest in a theocracy, the elected president in a democracy.

And now the four goal-directed elements:

The *creed* of the leading institution is the philosophy of the society, accepted by all but often only dimly or emotionally understood. It is the creed which determines what shall be judged right and also what will be available to feeling. Some examples: the Nicene Creed adopted in Constantinople in A.D. 381; the Magna Carta forced on King John by the English barons at Runnymede in 1215; the third Constitution presented to the Eighth Congress of Soviets of the U.S.S.R. by Comrade Stalin on November 25, 1936 (but never followed).

The *accounts* of the leading institution contain the myths of the society, those fundamental stories which contain the beliefs which are judged basic by the whole society; for example, the Bible of the Jews, the Vedic Hymns of the Hindus, the Iliad and Odyssey of the Greeks, the New Testament of the Christians.

The *style* of the leading institution is made up of the fashions followed by the aristocracy, not only in clothes, as the word has come to imply, but also in mannerisms, in attitudes, in beliefs. Style is the quality of an institution which displays itself in the form of actions as a way of conveying meanings apart from the actions themselves.

Finally, the *aim* of the leading institution is that set for the entire society as its ultimate goal. The aim could be, for instance, the perfection of society in the future as provided by the experimental sciences, or it could be life after death as guaranteed by a religion.

The last four items: creed, myth, style and aim, may be given a cover term. It will be convenient to lump them together under the word *value*, furnished to a society by the leading institution.

The Institutional Environment

Institutions, not surprisingly, have deep and lasting effects: in the

laying down of habits of action, in the selection of personal preferences, in the formation of beliefs.

The introduction of the individual to the institutions among
which he will spend the greater part of his adult life occurs with no
great ceremony. He has in many cases already prepared himself for
the one in which he will earn his living, and he has become more or
less automatically a member of the others. He registers to vote, he
pays taxes, and so begins to take part in politics; he marries and so
enters into the compact of the family; he joins a golf club, buys a car.
The chances are that he was already a member of some religion,
usually that of his parents.

The individual as a matter of fact participates in most of the
institutions in his society and is not merely a member of some of
them. All institutions affect him, though in a falling-off series of
importance; no one can be said to be completely in touch with the
influences from his society which play upon him until he has
visited all its significant corners; among others, for example, a
slaughterhouse and the children's ward of a hospital.

From now on the stimuli for his basic tissue needs will come
from institutions. Subject to the occupational hazards peculiar to the
institution of his choice and aimed chiefly at the rewards obtainable
thereby, he will become an institutional man. He will, like the lower
animals, make the responses he is stimulated to make; only, in his
case those responses will be institutional.

For instance the drive to survive can be turned from avoidance
to excitatory behavior by switching the concept of death from
punishment to reward. The prospect of death is an occasion for
anxiety when considered as the end of human life, but it can serve to
reduce a need if it is considered the beginning of survival of another
sort for an immortal soul. Nobody worries about death who consid-
ers it only a stage on the way.

Institutions taken together constitute a social environment.
They furnish the individual with what his needs indicate he must
have, usually at the rate of one per institution. The law of society is
that the response exceeds the stimulus in at least a sufficient number
of cases to insure the development of an apparatus to provide the

stimulus, with the results that later stimulations will be more refined and meet with more elaborate responses. The apparatus is handed on from one generation to the next. Hence we have anciently-established churches, stable governments, classics in art, and the accumulated knowledge and techniques resulting from scientific investigations.

Stimuli of one sort or another often penetrate the individual without being noticed; they may even pass through his consciousness without receiving much attention. He is in a sense unaware of them. The vaguer and more general the stimulation the more likely this is to be true. Institutional conditioning is largely unconscious conditioning. What lies beyond the individual's range of vision lies also beyond his control, and so in many instances when he thinks he is exercising an arbitrary choice it may happen that he is merely acting in response to a stimulus.

The individual is under the control of institutions all the more because he is unaware of their influence over him. They impose a uniformity upon him which insures that the actions which result from his deliberations are guided by motives deeply held and socially prevalent and therefore not inclined to upset customary ways of thinking, feeling and acting.

Beliefs of all degrees of strength exist, from those brief and fleeting thoughts which the individual entertains momentarily and then dismisses, to the more fundamental and stable dogmas which he holds so deeply that to question them would mean to challenge his very sanity.

It is this last group to which I wish to direct attention. The fundamental beliefs concern the very nature of existence, and they are held unconsciously — that is to say, without the individual knowing that he holds them. They rise to the surface only at the moment when he is called on for actions which depend upon them, and that is why in critical situations he often behaves in ways which surprise even him.

There are as a matter of fact two separate and distinct sets of fundamental beliefs lodged in the unconscious mind of every individual: those which are the result of his membership in a social group, and those which result from his own personal experiences. We may call the first set of beliefs public; the second private. Private beliefs may or may not conform to public beliefs, but it is the public beliefs which govern most of the individual's actions and must do so as long as he remains a member of his society. Obviously, the kind of public belief which keep hungry people in India from eating cows is absent in the Americans who eat them.

The First Amendment to the Constitution of the United States, adopted in 1791, recites that Congress shall make no laws prohibiting the free exercise of religion. Section Two of Chapter One, Article 59-7, of the Criminal Code of the Soviet Union lists religious propaganda among the crimes against the State.

Public beliefs are dictated by institutions, especially by the leading institution which decides what the members of a particular society shall hold most important. In the unconscious, then, it is the social part whose contents are determined by the leading institution, which exercises control over individual behavior by means of approvals and restraints.

There is always a minority of dissidents who disagree with the authorities no matter what the system of belief, and who tend to put their own experiences ahead of those of society. They come from two groups: those who are incapable of understanding the public beliefs, and those who have beliefs of their own they would like the public to adopt. The former are weaker than usual: the idiots, if you like; and the latter are stronger: the geniuses. The former group is of course always the larger. The leading institution in western civilization is experimental science, and there are always those who refuse to accept its findings. There still exists a Flat Earth Society whose members hold regular meetings and pass solemn resolutions.

But for most purposes the individual is integrated into his society by his unconscious acceptance of its beliefs. Because public beliefs are held in common, the individual feels more secure with them; he not only believes what the other members of his society believe, he also thinks, feels and acts as they do. Many of these beliefs are false, but, carried out in practice, they are often as effective as true ones, at least temporarily. Men are more often than not the prisoners of programs which prove how perilous consistency in a system with inadequate premises can be in practice.

If it is the case that ultimately the truth shall prevail, "ultimately" is a very long time. Meanwhile men are motivated and happenings brought about as the consequences of false beliefs. Things go wrong as often as they do is because of partly false information leading to emotional preferences and conflicting desires.

Although institutions are hard to live with, no other way has been found to deal with large populations. Still there is the private side of the individual, his reasoning powers, his hopes, his fears, his dreams, all of which must be reserved to him in the midst of his social obligations and institutional connections. Word often comes from Russian prison camps that what men feel most keenly besides the tortures and deprivations is the lack of solitude. Abram Tertz, a Soviet writer imprisoned for his dissident views, has given a good account of what it feels like never to be alone.

The dignity of the individual is a difficult thing to maintain. Rare is the government that offers it no interference; the ordinary conditions of life present a strong enough challenge. Most people have to work for a living, and while that in itself is nothing to pity them for, most have to work much too hard. Labor in excess is dehumanizing, whether in overlong hours on a farm or monotonous operations in a factory; and under whatever political system.

In countries where there is still some measure of freedom, the private life of the individual is protected in many ways, and it is left to him to determine how he will occupy his time during periods of leisure in order to supplement the work of institutions.

The attitude toward leisure is urgently in need of reconsideration now that it promises to become a more general possession, no longer the exclusive preserve of the wealthy. The reduction in the number of working hours and days makes of it a common practice in the heavily industralized countries; many official holidays are now common in business; and early retirement is becoming more and more common.

Over and above the institutional requirements, there remains the spectacle of the stubborn individual who in the last analysis is his own man or woman. He belongs to himself exclusively, in asserting his own personality. But it would be a mistake to consider this merely as freedom from the demands of work. No laziness is implied but something wider and deeper: a kind of intense passivity. Laziness is merely the desire to perform some other kind of work, and the uses of leisure frequently mean that an individual employed in one institution moves into another for his recreation. The medical practitioner becomes a "Sunday painter" or goes fishing.

In being tenaciously himself the individual's privacy is always involved. His last preserve is the inward area of his personal beliefs, even if some of these might happen to be false. His task therefore is to defend his private life while leading a public one, of preserving his preferences sometimes merely because they are his and no one else's, and of identifying himself with his uniqueness which should not be lost in the public shuffle because of what it is worth to him.

Chapter IX
The Domain of Cultures

From Institutions to Cultures

We noted in previous chapters how the effort to meet individual needs leads to the formation of institutions. Now we must see how institutions in their turn lead to the organizations of cultures.

Although needs are common to all individuals, behavior patterns laid down by the drives to obtain satisfactions vary from culture to culture. A culture is what results from the rearrangement man has made in his material environment by means of interacting institutions. Just how and what is rearranged determines the character of the culture. Anyone who has travelled to a distant land and noted the differences in its customs and language, its traditions and beliefs, would understand the meaning of culture.

A culture is a large and a loose organization but it is indivisible. Two institutions of different kinds have more in common if they are parts of the same culture than two institutions of the same kind in different cultures.

Culture is the name for the values of a society, incorporated in those material things it holds most important. The word must be used to include not only the values but the ways in which the values determine how the aims of the society are approached.

Every society has a culture which is to a large extent unique. The uniqueness is apparent in the ways in which its institutions differ from similar institutions in other cultures. Peculiar cultural customs are not products of chance but of ecological adaptations.

* * *

With this distinction in mind let us examine the list of institutions in order to see what each contributes.

The composition of the *family* is often different in different cultures. How many wives to a family, how many husbands? Who dominates, the husband or the wife? How much of the life of the culture is conducted in the home, how much in the marketplace?

In each society, of course, the prevailing way of doing things is considered the normal way; and anyone who wants to learn about human nature must first recognize that any arrangement works as well as any other provided that it is established and has survived for more than a single generation.

The Chinese for thousands of years centered their culture on the family and life at home, though this is now in process of being changed. For the ancient Greeks, to take the opposite extreme, family life was not as important as social life, the life of the city. Greek society was almost exclusively male. Women were not encouraged to read and write, to assume responsibilities, or to take part in any large-scale cultural activities, such as government or the arts.

Next let us consider *education*. The more advanced the culture the more knowledge it possesses, and of course the character of the knowledge as well as its extent differs from culture to culture. The knowledge peculiar to a culture must be passed on to the members of its new generation. Each culture has its own methods for doing this, its own teachers. Education has never been the institution to dominate a culture, even though the ancient Chinese and the modern Europeans have given it a high place.

The information which education transmits is of utmost importance to the young. It is here that cultural conditioning begins. Already in the cradle, babies are fed the elements of belief in a particular system of ideas, and, though no one calls it that, it is the one dominating the culture. The ideas remain thereafter in the unconscious parts of adult minds, where they can be revived by memory (but without being remembered) and dictate many of the individual's thoughts, feelings and actions. The baby is in fact the innocent recipient of the beliefs which its chance appearance in particular culture has determined for it.

Severe differences in *economic* practices exist from culture to culture. The production and exchange of material goods naturally depends upon what is produced and how the exchange takes place. Some cultures have done well with a low production of food, clothing and shelter, and few extras. In other cultures the variety has been elaborate.

In the manner of exchange, the varieties run all the way from barter — the direct exchange of one kind of goods for another — to the more familiar medium of coins or paper money. We are now in process of testing a third and new method, based on the transfer of credit and debit entries without the use of cash.

I cannot leave this topic without mentioning a crucial issue: the ownership of the means of production: property. In the older monarchies and modern democracies the custom has been established of depending upon private ownership — in a word, capitalism. This can be absolute or modified. A socialist is a capitalist who has given up all hope of ever personally having large amounts of money.

In some countries, Sweden, for instance, the ownership of a factory by the laborers who work in it is being tried. In the United States the large pension fund of a labor union may hold large amounts of stock in the company. In the Soviet Union and Communist China the state is the sole owner of all the means of production, farms and factories alike.

At this stage of things it is clear that the profit motive leads to more individual initiative, and hence to a more efficient system, than does the vast bureaucracy of a socialist state. The United States is more productive and more prosperous than the Soviet Union. How these differences will be resolved it is difficult to say.

Transportation is usually a low-level institution because it makes few claims of its own and exists chiefly to serve other institutions. Its importance, however, is an index to the complexity of the culture: when there are more goods to move about, and when individuals have to travel often in the course of performing their social duties, transportation becomes more important.

Any institution can get out of hand. In the United States in 1973 with its 210 million people there were 89,781,000 motor cars and 21,397,000 trucks in use. In 1976 Americans bought 10,098,173 new cars, a commitment to one form of transportation of monumental proportions, for this figure is in addition to those of other forms: trains were still running and airplanes moved enormous numbers of people.

In a scientific-industrial culture such as our own, transportation makes tremendous strides in efficiency thanks to the workings of technology. There are few times when many people are not engaged in coming and going.

The chief vehicle (though by no means the only one) of *communication* is language. Cultures vary with respect to their languages; they vary also with respect to the amount and flow of information. A large amount of information and a high rate of flow indicates a high level of culture.

It is a startling fact that a natural or colloquial language is the largest artifact ever invented. The English language contains more than half a million words, and more people must have been involved in its construction than in anything else. Language is a service institution; no other institution could get along without it.

In the literary arts, however, it is a constitutive affair, for literature relies to some extent upon the natural rhythms of language. Old languages are also depositories of the values of cultures, values imbedded in turns of speech an idioms as well as in old folks beliefs and sayings.

Newcomers to the cultural scene, only some three hundred years old, the *pure sciences* have taken their place near the top in the list of influential institutions because they serve the others in many important ways. As a result of the discovery of the experimental laboratory method of checking hypotheses, science has nourished technology, expanded our knowledge of the total environment, and finally altered the institutions of philosophy and religion almost beyond recognition.

One of the largest lessons to be learned from experimental, science is that the list of institutions may not have been exhausted. If after many thousands of years we can still come across one which is so powerful, perhaps others more powerful still await discovery.

Technology differs from culture to culture as much as anything does: the utensils employed in eating, for instance; but the distinction of course cuts deeper than that, for I am talking here about artifacts in general. Any history of technology discloses surprising differences in the ways in which people have met ordinary tasks and in the artifacts they have employed to these ends.

There are obvious similarities, too; the chairs found in Tutankhamen's tomb, put there in the 14th century B.C., are much like our own. But a comparison of the tomb itself with one of ours today shows that the differences are greater than the similarities.

Culture cannot be confined to any one enterprise; it involves the entire range of organized human activities, and none of these can be conducted without instruments of some sort. There is no institution which does not employ a vigorous technology; indeed each has its own. But they do interact; the discovery of new materials for industrial and military purposes has also furthered the fine arts. New materials, such as heat-resistant ceramics, invented for the nose cones of rockets, are now used by painters and sculptors.

That the *fine arts* differ from culture to culture is a point which must be obvious to anyone who has travelled extensively or looked at the remains of ancient cultures. Art serve cultures in two ways: by intensifing the sensory experience of individual members and by embodying values in an enduring way. Both are of supreme importance, of greater importance than the word "entertainment," so prevalent now, would indicate.

The *decorative arts*, which apply the findings of the fine arts to other institutions, to the embellishment of architecture, to the interior of buildings, to rugs and draperies, furniture and clothing, for instance, differ markedly from culture to culture. They are, one might say, the popular, prevalent side of the fine arts. If it is true that environment determines behavior then decoration plays a larger role in human life than has been recognized.

Higher Institutions

The next four institutions represent the efforts of man to reach beyond the institutional level, beyond even the state; they are the activities of culture in the strict sense: man attempting to rise above the immediate requirements of survival. Through the fine arts, the pure sciences, philosophies and religions, culture provides avenues for man's emancipation from the finite cycle of organic life.

The great importance of the higher institutions is that while they are products of culture they are not culture-bound. They enable the individual to strive to get outside the culture to some extent. At the same time they provide a cover by containing that striving within admissible limits.

In the attempt to account for everything by means of a system of ideas wider than any other, *philosophies* finds their greatest application when a particular philosophy is embodied in a leading institution, such as a religion spread by a church. Of course a philosophy need not be religious to be important.

It is less well recognized that secular societies also depend upon official philosophies. The Soviet Union and Communist China have both adopted varieties of the political philosophy of Marxism, however serious its shortcomings. The government of the United States as embodied in its Constitution utilizes the philosophical ideas of an Englishman, John Locke, and a Frenchman, Charles-Louis de Secondat, Baron de la Brède et de Montesquieu. Though philosophy is poorly regarded in the United States today, its effects are felt widely. While firmly believing that philosophy does not count, the average American citizen practices a philosophy without knowing that he does so. The one that he commonly practices is an uneasy combination of idealism and materialism, the idealism of those who know that things are not as they ought to be, and the materialism of those who suppose that as things ought to be so they are. The result is a certain number of inconsistent actions which are partly self-defeating.

To the extent to which the varied institutions and activities of a society are consistent, that society is effective. A society internally inconsistent is bound to reveal in practice the weakness of disorganization. If it holds together, common elements must be responsible.

There are no advanced cultures in which philosophy does not play an important and even crucial part, if the ability of reason to organize society on the basis of a system of ideas is recognized as a philosophical effort. Only philosophy lies at a sufficiently deep level to operate in this fashion, and its ability to dominate is enhanced by its invisibility.

Religions differ from culture to culture. Every culture has its own religion, and many have tried to extend their domain beyond the particular society in which they originated. The standard examples of religions which have sought global domination are Hinduism, Buddhism, Christianity and Islam. I have left out the Confucians who were never that strong, and Judaism, as old as any, which was never that large.

Religions as institutions are combinations of many things: a creed, a philosophy to defend it, a ritual to embody it, and a church with its clergy to supervise and sometimes to compel conformity to it.

Weber has pointed out that in practice all religions seem to share a common notion that some form of suffering will lead to salvation. In this way they combine the feelings and the reason, eventually relying upon the emotional acceptance of a creed and a ritual to reinforce that acceptance. It is well to remember, however, that when men seek to identify themselves with God, it is not entirely in the interest of God.

The religious spirit of man dictates one sort of reaction, the church fosters quite another. To the religious spirit, in Max Weber's words, "senseless death has seemed only to put the decisive stamp upon the senselessness of life itself."

If religious inquiry and astronomical findings tell us anything, it is that we are not a party to the process. We are admonished to "Praise the Lord", but for what? For granting us the glory of existence, or for taking it away? Most churches would deny this view and substitute for it explanations which appeal to the feelings and neither to the reason nor the facts. Consider for example the ways in which different religions have provided for the constancy of man's opposite aims: how to achieve oblivion (Hinayana Buddhism) and how to achieve personal immortality (Christianity).

The contradictions, however, are not only *between* religions, they are also *within* religions. While Buddha sought to achieve oblivion, Buddhism promised immortal life. And while Jesus came to preach the end of the world, Christianity became a way of continuing in it.

Neither science nor religion can answer the ultimate questions. The individual has to learn how to live with the fact that the issues which concern him most cannot be solved by institutions, for they make only questionable answers to such unanswerable questions as the origins of the universe, the existence of the gods, the purpose of human life.

* * *

An individual in the course of his life in a culture will make contact with, and either serve or be served by, every one of its institutions; and not at random, for just as the institutions are arranged in an order peculiar to the culture, so the individual's participation in them is ordered also. They make relatively different demands upon him, and he in turn expects different things from them.

The rigidity or flexibility of the institutions and of the relations between them determines the extent to which a culture is growing or declining. Cultures rarely remain the same over long periods of time, however much they often seem to be unchanging. Often when there are no visible signs of change the factors compelling it are quietly assembling unnoticed, and have their dynamic effects later.

The State as Institution

In the discussion of the various institutions which together make up a culture, I only touched on politics which, because of its omnipresence, requires special attention. Politics, in the form of the state or nation, is the social institution which, by means of its laws, regulates not only all other institutions but also all individuals. Its influence permeates every corner. The laws governing a society are derived from the state; the state is an establishment of morality; and morality is a product of an urgency promoted by circumstances. No state, then no order; no order, then no hope of need-reduction for the individual because social cooperation calls for the regulation of competition to prevent total frustration.

No states are alike, not even when they profess to have the same form of government. There is a difference between an absolute monarch and one who is answerable to nobles and lords. The democracy of Great Britain is not the same as the one practiced in France. These differences reach into the lives of individual citizens.

What the state accomplishes it does by reserving exclusively to itself the use of force within a given territory, as Weber pointed out. It has the task of preserving order in the culture, and thus ideally exerts more of a regulative then a substantive function, though of course it is quite capable of getting out of hand and determining virtually everything. In the Soviet Union and Communist China today the state makes all the substantive decisions, and citizens are allowed to take only those actions of which it does not specifically disapprove. It thus becomes a senior partner in the activities of every institution and is not merely one among many as it is in the democracy of the United States or of Great Britain.

In every case the state utilizes a particular philosophy and a particular morality to regulate and enforce compliance with the established order by means of enacted laws, with police to maintain the order and an army to defend it. The tasks of maintaining order and of defending the state lend themselves to excesses which are so common that they can hardly be regarded as abnormal. The repressive police state, in which individual liberties are suspended — or held not to exist — has had a long history. A state which threatens others is merely showing its size and power.

Many of the sufferings of mankind are due to the deliberate actions of mankind. So long as it remains true that man's nature is to exceed himself, few individuals will be able to lead tranquil lives and no state will be permanently peaceful. Five thousand years of human history tell us that the fighting of wars destroys the arts of peace, that human nature contains a basic conflict which must be eradicated if we are to progress to the point where everything we do, every step we take, every effort we make, benefits us as a species. Human nature has changed in many respects but it has yet to change in this one.

Legal systems of course differ from state to state. The system of common law which prevails in Great Britain and the United States is not the same as the system of French law, but all three have more in common than either has with laws and courts in the Soviet Union. The state reserves to itself the exclusive right of taxation, which is the practice of withdrawing from the total economy the amounts deemed necessary. The amounts vary, depending upon the type of state and the degree of its regulation of citizens and institutions.

The social group belonging to the state operates as a bureaucracy. The larger the population, the larger the bureaucracy required. Of course everything depends upon the degree of regulation sought by the state. Twenty years ago, when the population of the United States was smaller, the bureaucracy was smaller. Now it has become disproportionately larger, a force of its own, and is neither regulated nor controlled.

The bureaucracy is so large in so many governments today — as true in the Soviet Union and Communist China as it is in the United States — that in many ways its excesses are paralyzing. It represents the triumph of officials over innovators. The introduction of anything new is not considered by existing administrators a sign of progress but a challenge. The domination of a bureaucracy means that nothing new can be added to the society; it is considered good enough if what has been done can be consolidated. The reverse of this is of course confining innovation only to administration, so that new kinds of regulation are regarded as signs of progress.

On the whole, geniuses are bad for institutions. Mediocrity is sometimes the proper name for a jealous majority. The work of a solitary genius may not be enough to upset the established order, but his presence is a constant reminder of everyone else's incapacity, which is why no innovative philosophy could get a hearing in a state like the Soviet Union today.

The rise and domination of the bureaucracy in large countries is due perhaps to a single development: the enormous and rapid increase in population. More people to regulate means more regulation, until the increase in laws and statutes almost spins out of control and people seem to bureaucrats to be only opportunities for regulation.

In the United States in 1976 there were two thousand different federal agencies, together they issued 7000 new regulations, many of which were overlapping and contradictory. As many as sixty of these agencies were concerned with the making of rules governing the production and distribution of various forms of energy.

Another good example of bureaucracy comes from higher education. American universities formerly had two aims: communicating existing knowledge and adding to it. Now they exist chiefly in order to be administered. The phenomenon of layered administrators: provosts, assistant provosts, deans and assistant deans, all with vast clerical staffs, constitute a new academic bureaucracy. The added cost of operation does not materially increase productivity.

What we are faced with throughout our society as a result of this movement is not the "dictatorship of the working class" as predicted by Marx but a dictatorship of the bureaucracy. This is certainly true in the Soviet Union where the members of the Communist Party, strictly limited in number, are the bureaucrats. It is not yet true in the United States, where the industrialists still hold a precarious lead.

Institutions under a given mandate tend to be restless and to seek to extend their influence. A certain amount of power-seeking can be allowed provided it is regulated, but an excess must be cut off. That is why democracies always have checks and balances to guarantee that the society is not frozen in place but also to see that it does not spin out of control altogether. The state has the dual task of facilitating and of regulating — and of not permitting the one to usurp the legitimate claims of the other. There cannot ever be too many facilitative laws or too few restrictive ones.

I cannot leave this topic without pointing out one of the methods by which institutions are welded into cultures. An outstanding leader from one institution often finds his followers among others. Many observers of human nature have pointed to the deep urge of most people to follow a leader. This can be either because of the faith they have in his extraordinary personal qualities or because of the character of his exceptional accomplishments. Every public figure is an actor with a limited repertory who plays only himself. What Hegel has called "the world-historical individual" and Weber described as "the charismatic leader" are usually men active in politics, Alexander the Great, for instance, or Napoleon. Paradoxically such men are revered in their lifetimes and for centuries after because of the number of people they succeeded in getting killed. Political leaders are nearly always "war lords", and their memories kept sacred. The destructive effects of their actions are quickly forgotten, indeed the public forgets everything in a few years. How else could politicians continue in office and soldiers make reputations?

It is a lucky thing that the effects which wars leave in their wake are not altogether destructive. When the brutal storms they have raised subside, there is often a residue of positive effects. World-historical individuals are sometimes followed by gains. Alexander brought about a Hellenized Asia, Napoleon cleared the way in Europe for the rise of democracies.

What is not often remembered is that leaders can move great numbers of people only in the direction in which they had already wished to go. The evidence that the individual's drives are more vigorous and more demanding than can be provided for is contained in the series of disastrous conflicts and revolutions which sweep away everything constructive which had been so sedulously erected and so carefully preserved through the years.

When India was officially granted her independence by the British on August 14, 1947, Hindus and Moslems on the border of the newly-created state of Pakistan slaughtered each other. Murder, rapine and arson accounted for more than a million people, all in the name of religion. How old were the ruins of the ancient Cambodian city of Angkor Wat when in the 1960s the Vietnamese war swept over it?

Nothing internal to the individual or external to him is stronger than his drive to dominate the environment, particularly in its negative phase in which it can be reduced only through destruction. It is the secret ambition of every dictator to rule over a population of clones.

Whatever can be provided for human comfort and security can be annihilated with equal efficiency. In relatively quiet periods when the only human needs seem to be for knowledge and enjoyment, the need to do, under its violent aspect of the need to destroy, is almost forgotten, and men tend to think of themselves as creatures of good will, oblivious of the fact that when the good will is dominant there is still an ill will which is for the time being recessive.

While leaders of good will usually have less effect upon their contemporaries, they have much more upon the members of successive generations. They come from the arts and the sciences, a Johann Sebastian Bach and a Rembrandt, an Isaac Newton and an Einstein, and what they accomplish continue to be of benefit to society. If we remember that the list includes architects and technologists, then we can recognize that the building of cultures is the work of such men.

Einstein once observed in conversation that there were two Germanies, the Germany of the gentle humanists, of Heine and Goethe, Mozart and Brahms; and the other Germany of Hitler and the Nazis. Both represented forces, he said, that were deeply imbedded in the society. But if the same two tendencies co-exist in every society, as I believe that they do, it only shows the basic conflict that lies within human nature itself.

The Citizen

I have talked about the individual as a member of a social group, for in relation to the state this is his chief function. Yet everything that has been accomplished for societies had its point of origin at some time and place in the mind of a single individual. I do not wish to deny that fact, only to extend it to its effects on social organizations which require the permissive compliance, if not the cooperation, of the state itself.

When we draw a distinction between individual and group behavior, we must recognize that the individual tends to be dominated not only by special interests but also by emotional prejudices. The social group has its customs and traditions, its deep-seated beliefs, and it tends to reject with scorn and even with violence the customs and beliefs of others. Here the state must decide just what degree of dissent is permitted, always on the assumption that if the dissident minority grows into a large majority a change is demanded.

The cultural variation with respect to legitimate dissent varies widely. In the Soviet Union and Communist China there is no such thing; dissidents are sent to labor camps, or to hospitals for the insane where they are given drugs which permanently damage their minds.

By way of contrast, in social democracies like the United States and Great Britain, individual freedoms of thought and expression prevail and no such cruel repressions are practiced. Freedom from want must not be allowed to exclude the right to express different opinions, to change jobs, or to leave the country. In the last analysis the preservation of the dignity of the individual rests on the practice of retaining reason and fact as a final court of appeal. This is the only minimal faith acceptable, for it means trusting conclusions based on evidence from the disclosures of sense experience.

We all look up to the "man of principle", but what if he acts from the wrong principles? In that case we have to take the risk, because actions without principles are unacceptable. The only totally free society would be the one in which the only principle was that there were no other principles. But then that would not be a free society because it would not be a society. The individual will always judge a society to be free if he is in absolute agreement with the practice of its principles, whatever the principles. This is the case with most of the individuals in Asian countries. They have so little experience of freedom that I doubt most of them would know what I am talking about.

Those of us who live in western democracies, Europeans and Americans chiefly, do not recognize how lucky we are and how rare the circumstances that allow us our freedoms. At certain periods a broadly based democracy was known to the ancient Greeks and Romans but rarely since then.

More common is the institution of slavery, which has not always carried that name. Many varieties of slavery have existed in the world at one time or another. In ancient Greece and Rome slaves belonged to individuals. Now whole populations are enslaved by the state. No other interpretation can be put upon the restrictions of the ordinary citizen in the Soviet Union which certainly make of him an industrial serf.

It is a rare age indeed when individuals enjoy the freedom to think and speak as they wish, even to start institutions. In the Middle Ages the firm grip of Christianity, in the form of the Roman Catholic Church in the west and the Greek Orthodox Christian Church in the east, stifled the freedoms. Today in Asia, with the Soviet Union and Communist China, this is happening again. If Asian communism should spread to the west, we could go back again into a dark night of absolutism of the kind that existed during the Middle Ages. Nothing does more harm to political freedom and speculative thought than an official philosophy, and that is what Communist countries have now.

When such systems of ideas as Marxism are accepted emotionally as the absolute truth, wars are fought over them and the most horrible cruelties are practiced. A convinced believer is one who because of his absolute faith cannot even conceive of the possibility that anything about his philosophy is wrong and so what he offers to others is agreement or death.

The Cultural Environment

Everyone lives in a state or nation, a political organization which is ever present. Everyone lives also in a cultural environment, but it is possible to distinguish between a state and a culture. The state is part of the culture but is very far from constituting all of it.

A Viking culture existed as early as the eighth and ninth centuries when there were no Scandinavian states. Long before the kingdoms of Norway, Denmark and Sweden, a common language and a common religion held the people together. Culture is indivisible because everyone is culturally conditioned. The individual conforms to a particular culture so completely that often two individuals from different cultures seem not to be the same animal. That is why it is fair to demand of any explanation of human nature that it include an understanding of the effects of sharing in all of the activities of society — its workings and achievements, its failures.

The cultivated individual is one who is fully aware of all the forces that play upon his times, who has heightened his sensitivity by prolonged and intensive exposure to the arts, extended his horizons by intimate acquaintance with the findings of the sciences, deepened his knowledge by a reading of history, and expanded his sympathies by feelings for the tribulations and trials of others.

What is a cultural environment exactly? That mixture of customs and traditions, of artifacts and institutions, which have accumulated independently and which so surround the individual in his daily life that he interacts at every level.

We have noted that every culture is dominated by a set of beliefs and governed by a system of morality which dictates what is expected of the behavior of individuals. What we must add now is that such beliefs and moralities differ from culture to culture and thus make different kinds of demands upon their members. Chief among these perhaps is the set of beliefs which, as we have noted, has been accepted socially at so deep a level that its presence tends to be forgotten. Unconsciously held ideas are the binding agents and chief influences in the cultural environment, for they determine the thoughts, feelings and actions of every individual.

The highest level of social structure and control is the established morality of the society. Religion, which once was the official custodian of the established morality, speaks more often for another world than for this one, while the lower levels of economics and politics are insufficient to furnish the aims of society as a whole. Morality, the strongest single element in the cultural environment, is a product of the institution of philosophy where the speculative alternatives in ethical theories and moral problems are entertained.

The social group is one of the largest and most potent factors in the cultural environment of the individual but by no means the only one. For there is the whole collection of artifacts peculiar to the culture. We have looked at artifacts many times. Here I want merely to point out the cultural differences. We noted earlier that artifacts differ markedly from culture to culture. What we did not note was the peculiar way in which artifacts acquire more uses in a given culture than the one for which they were originally designed. They begin as tools and instruments with specialized uses but acquire others; they have an existence of their own and can be employed in ways not originally intended; above all they can have unforeseen effects on behavior.

Radio antennas were designed to aid in wartime ground communication, but a scientist at the Bell Telephone Laboratories turned one toward the sky and to his astonishment it continued to receive signals. He had found a new use for it — and radio astronomy was born.

There are other instruments of war which were used for peaceful purposes: the airplane, first employed for bombing, became a means of peaceful transportation; atomic energy, developed as a weapon, is now helpful in the treatment of cancer.

Artifacts are parts of the cultural environment and lead "lives" of their own. In so doing they have multiple effects, neither foreseen nor intended; some favorable, other deleterious. The pollution of the environment is an undesirable result of the successful use of physical and chemical forms of energy. The waste products of nuclear energy are difficult to destroy, and many resulting from chemical manufacture have poisoned the rivers.

It is important to remember, however, that we never altogether lose the human individual in his cultural relations. Despite the social groups and artifacts with which he must reckon, he has an authentic existence of his own. He may be a technical expert in an institution, but beyond that he may also have his own aim, a requirement that is more broadly spaced. There are values beyond the institution, beyond even the collection of institutions, with which he can make himself familiar. Along with his autonomy we have noted elements within him which collectively threaten his security. We have learned to know a lot about him that is none too pleasant. Undesirable individual traits become reinforced and intensified when collected in units as large as states or nations. People can be organized as easily to destroy as to build; organized social welfare is common but so also is organized cruelty. Foreign aid vies in foreign policy with foreign wars. The ambivalence of aggression takes on a vicious form when it issues in anything as enormous and destructive as an international conflict. In the history of the human species peace has occupied only a series of brief intervals.

Clearly the problem is larger than the state, it is worldwide. Human nature sends out waves of effects which must be included in any analysis because they radiate back and are felt in the end by the individual.

Understanding human nature means understanding the largest of human organizations and the widest of consequences. Therefore, if we are to address ourselves to the whole human problem, we shall have to look at those collections of states which go under the name of civilizations.

Chapter X
The Global Environment

From Cultures to Civilizations

In the last chapter we noted what a culture is. Now the circle is being drawn wider. We began with the individual and without any break in the argument we find ourselves discussing civilizations as vast constructions made necessary by individual needs.

I begin by defining a civilization as that large and homogeneous unit which expands a culture beyond the confines of any single country or nation. Civilizations are the largest organizations we know of in which the whole to some extent determines the parts and in which the parts are inter-related. They are so large in fact and so widely spread that no one is much aware of them. Civilizations are not common in the history of mankind. In the whole range of history Toynbee was able to find only 21 examples of the species. Only 21 times, in other words, has a culture spread widely enough to constitute a civilization.

Few survive today. There is western civilization — Europe, the Americas, Australia and New Zealand. There is a civilization in India, which includes many of the countries in southeast Asia. There is a civilization in China, which extends to Korea and Formosa.

There is an Islamic civilization reaching from nations at the eastern end of the Mediterranean all the way to Pakistan. Many small cultures continue to exist but they are not sufficiently inclusive.

The individual rarely notices his civilization. He is more aware of the differences than the similarities, and the fact that he lives all his life as part of a vast organization receives little more attention from him than his breathing. He is aware only of being a citizen of a state, and unless he travels to a foreign country that is all he knows. His civilization is the whole of his world; he cannot imagine any other; its boundaries set limits to his vision; he seldom sees beyond them. When he first encounters others he views them with hostility and regards their customs as strange ways of doing things, their institutions as morally wrong.

In a word, he judges other civilizations by his own, which he holds to be the absolute standard. A very great effort on his part, and considerable experience, is required if he is to get outside this narrow point of view.

Civilizations are not static affairs, they come and go. They are known to have four career phases. According to the studies made by Toynbee and others they grow, they flourish, they break down, and they disintegrate. Each of these phases usually takes hundreds of years, so the chances are that an individual will live most of his life in some one of the four. He will not ordinarily know which one, because such movements are difficult if not impossible to detect at any moment in time. Yet his relations with the one to which he is totally committed by the accident of his birth will vary accordingly. In the growth and flourishing phases he will feel himself to be intimately involved, while in the breakdown and disintegration phases he will tend more to draw apart and fall back upon his own inner resources. Objective philosophies are fashionable in the first two phases, subjective philosophies in the last two; materialisms in the first, idealisms in the second.

Despite the inclusiveness of civilizations, there are elements of cultures which transcend them. Two in particular stand out: a few traits and some institutions.

There are certain practices which extend to the whole of the human species because they are global and are found throughout all of history. I can think of two with records as old as any: prostitution, and the false "science" of astrology. Recently another has come to join them: cigarettes. No culture has yet been discovered, primitive or civilized, in which cigarettes have not been welcome.

Some institutions have had the power to maintain themselves beyond the life span of a single civilization. One famous case is Plato's Academy, a school of graduate studies in philosophy founded in Athens in 385 B.C. It survived through several cultures, Greek, Macedonian and Roman, until it was closed by the Emperor Justinian in A.D. 529, almost a thousand years later.

Great literature is often more durable than the civilization that produced it. There is an interesting parallel between the way in which the Akkadians studied the literary classics of the Sumerians they had conquered and the way in which several thousand years later the Romans cherished the Greek literary classics after Greece had become only a small and relatively unimportant province of the vast Roman Empire.

More often than not an institution pays a price for survival, and later efforts to keep it alive have been successful only by sacrificing something of its fullness and quality. Look for example at what happened to the Olympic Games. Begun in 776 B.C. and a feature of ancient Greek civilization, the original version was not limited to competition between athletes but included musical and dramatic contests together with popular recitals of Homer. Now the Olympic Games are exclusively athletic contests.

International trade became increasingly effective as an institution when it moved from luxuries to necessities; from the spices, ivory and incense of the oriental caravans of the Middle Ages to the shiploads of wheat and corn of the modern Kansas farmlands.

What today are called the "multi-national corporations", based in the United States and Europe, extend western civilization to third-world countries. Exxon, General Electric, General Motors, International Telephone and Telegraph, International Business Machines, DuPont, are spreading the scientific-industrial culture in a way which to some extent at least transcends their profit-making proclivities.

A single example: in a small country, Sweden, 2,000 companies based in Great Britain, Holland, West Germany, Norway, Switzerland, Denmark, France, the United States and Italy, in 1976 employed a total of 100,850 local workers, all learning industrial technologies.

Doing business across national boundaries offers one type of hope for the future. Extending business as well as communication and transportation globally is a step in the right direction, and recognizes the true nature of the interests and sympathies of mankind even though it is not to the liking of those who operate behind the iron curtain countries. There trade with the west is encouraged and practiced even though not acknowledged.

Everyone in a sense is culture-bound. No one lives all alone in the world; each of us is a part of some culture our ancestors have made and which we and our contemporaries have inherited and modified by means of the invention and construction of artifacts.

The improvement in artifacts not only sustains man in all the drives to reduce his needs, it also enlarges his living space. As we noted earlier, the environment with which he interacts has been extended recently in a number of directions. His range now reaches not only downward to the bottom of the oceans but also outward to other bodies in the solar system: he has been to the moon and back and sent spacecrafts to Mars.

The study of man in relation to his environment reveals how much he has expanded not only his explorations but also his control. No doubt his ultimate aim is to construct for himself an ecological niche, a friendly habitat, out of the whole of the cosmic universe, and perhaps in this way to escape from his cultural bondage. There are limits of course. Thus far we do not have even a global culture, though constructing one will have to be the next step. Diogenes, a contemporary of Aristotle, may have been the first to proclaim himself a "citizen of the universe"; he will certainly not be the last.

Few astronomers doubt that life is a common occurrence throughout the universe. This must be some comfort to anyone who has seen the photographs of the earth taken from outer space, from the surface of the moon, for example, and noted the isolation and loneliness of the human situation. If an individual were to learn that life on many planets in other galaxies is a high probability, he would tend to see himself as a mere sample of intelligent life forms, and this might give him a feeling of greater security.

Efforts are currently being made to contact beings in other solar systems elsewhere in the universe of galaxies. If there are millions of suns in our own galaxy, the repetition of the conditions that exist on earth must be multiplied many times more than we can possibly imagine.

On the big radio telescopes in Australia and the Soviet Union as well as in the United States and Peru, time is being programmed to listen for messages that might have been sent to us from other civilizations far away. The difficulty is simply the distance; it is so far to the nearest star, Tau Ceti, that it would take many lifetimes to send an unmanned space vehicle there even if we possessed the necessary technology.

One Civilization, or Many?

The world is growing smaller. Toynbee and others have asked whether for the first time in the history of the human species one civilization is not about to overwhelm the others. Our western civilization, because of the enormous successes of its scientific-industrial culture, is tending to spread everywhere. The signs certainly do point in that direction at the moment, but prediction is difficult because the number of variables involved exceeds our powers of calculation.

Would the establishment of a single global civilization be desirable? There are advantages and disadvantages to this prospect. Let us look first at the advantages.

The largest of these would be the establishment of a global order, with its elimination of wars and indeed of all armed conflict: peace on earth. Already there exist developments which tie nations together. Transportation and communication now have the technology to go very quickly right round the world. The use of the airplane for transportation is widespread; the fastest airplanes can reach anywhere on the globe in a few hours. As for communication, the telephone, the radio and television are worldwide, especially now that the messages are bounced off artificial satellites.

Although at the present time there exists no global language capable of being understood by everyone within the reach of radio, television does offer a common language: everyone is able to see pictures.

All mankind constitutes a single animal species because any two members of it can breed true despite their cultural differences. Consider also the widespread similarities of mental illnesses. Evidently types of disturbed behavior, labelled "abnormalities," have striking resemblances in very different civilizations. Certain uniform varieties of afflictions beset all members of the species.

The similarities between any two individuals are in the end greater than their differences, chiefly because there is only one kind of human individual and all possess the same set of organic needs. And the organic needs lead, not surprisingly, to the establishment of the same kinds of institutions. Thus the possibility of satisfying everyone by means of a common culture exists, though just exactly which culture that would be is not known at the present time.

* * *

So much for the advantages of a single global civilization, now for the disadvantages.

The most prominent of these is the monotony that would follow its establishment. There is a certain richness in difference that we can ill afford to lose. Consider the arts, for example. Of the many schools of painting, eastern and western, each contributes something to the appreciation of the values of existence. The same case can be made for all other culture traits. Who would wish to choose one kind of cuisine and eliminate the others? That would impoverish us all.

Perhaps the greatest of disadvantages is contained in the fact that any culture can decline, or, even worse, go bad. The great heights to which European civilization rose through the efforts of its artists and scientists was matched by the depths to which it fell in its endless wars. If such destruction could happen to one great civilization it could happen to any, and if there were only one, that would mean the end of the human species as we have known it.

There are other possible disadvantages to a single civilization. It may be for instance that the uninterrupted improvement in technology may mean more of a loss than a gain. We saw the advantages of the new technology in transportation and communication, now let us look at some of the disadvantages.

Transportation makes it possible today for the average traveler to cover thousands of miles in a matter of hours and visit many countries without receiving more than a few confused impressions. A popular trip to Europe for an American may number as many countries as days. An old anecdote has one young tourist remarking, "If today is Tuesday this must be Belgium."

The broadcasting in television is so good that the technology of the programs tends to dwarf the contents. Consider a crime serial in which the plots are similar from week to week and the outcome is identical: the detective always survives the threats to his life, and the criminal is always caught and presumably punished. There is more monotony than variety in such weekly programs, which thus have a dulling effect.

It would be fair to conclude from this that the medium often *defeats* the message. No Shakespeare of the screen has yet appeared. It is possible that in the end we shall be frustrated many times by the very artifacts that were designed to liberate us.

The Moral Outcome

We have been looking at human nature from many points of view but we have only touched on morality. It deserves a fuller treatment. It is part of human nature for the individual to think about what he ought to do and what restrains him.

Morality is so fundamental that it involves the way any two

individuals are bonded together. The question of morality can hardly be avoided, for every individual in the world effects continual interchanges with it. In so doing he is privileged to take advantage of opportunities for many need-satisfactions, but he also incurs obligations. He is free but he is also bound.

I said at the beginning of this book that what is needed is good; now we can turn that around and declare that the good is what is needed, but this time with the provision that what is organizing is good, what is disorganizing bad.

Morality involves privileges and obligations; also rights and duties. If you look closely you will see that there are four grades of morality resulting from the four different levels of organization. The individual is first of all himself, he is also a member of society; he belongs to a particular animal species; and he lives in the cosmic universe. Let us look briefly at each of these grades.

The first grade of morality is the individual grade. The individual in virtue of his existence has a moral obligation to himself to maintain his dignity, and he is responsible for his own integrity. He has of course to satisfy his organic needs and support his personality. To accomplish these ends he must deal with his environment appropriately so that in interchanges with it he can meet his obligations.

He must adjust his parts among themselves if he is to be free to deal with the world. He has many other connections, with institutions in his society for example, but he can deal with them properly only if he is at home with himself.

I pointed out earlier that the drives do not stop when the needs are reduced, and I described this as excessive behavior. (Defective behavior is also a fault: not doing enough to reduce the needs.) Man is born neither good nor bad. He is born with the needs and with the urge to exceed the needs in his drives.

Now the needs in themselves are good, but when the drives exceed them they may have effects which are bad. Most actions are mixed. Those in which the element of good is larger than the bad are called good; those in which the bad is larger than the good are called bad.

When someone refers to "individual morality," he means what he would like to do that he thinks society would not approve. When he says "social morality," he means what he thinks his society expects of him. Yet there is more to it than that. Because there is no universally accepted morality every society expects different things from its members. Every individual has his own set of desires, one of which may be for social approval.

After individual morality comes the second grade of morality, the social. Every individual is a member of some society, one among many. All individuals are attracted to all other individuals in virtue of a common dependence upon the society they share. Social morality therefore may be defined as the conduct of one individual toward another in consideration of their society.

Follow this through by multiplying the occasions, and a social ethics emerges. It may be described as the sum of the effects which a cohesive group of persons and artifacts exerts upon the conduct of an individual.

The aim of society is twofold. Its primary aim is to contribute to the next level of moral organization, humanity. Its secondary aim is to enable its individual members to achieve their own welfare. By behaving morally toward others the individual helps them to construct a society. Thus within the society there arises a morality whose members· expect everyone to behave in "correct," that is to say, socially approved, ways. This they accomplish through the establishment of rules of order and the enforcement of that order insofar as the rules and their enforcement are consistent with the stated aims.

The established morality of a society is not an arbitrary affair. Starting with the social ordering of the needs and drives, the morality is based upon how the majority thinks it can best cooperate with a view to achieving need-reductions, thus insuring its own survival. The society to which the individual belongs is a self-governing moral community. It is in the main inherited and thus exerts a formative influence upon him. He is molded by its peculiar structure, its materially productive forces, its unique properties. Its size is an elastic and vague affair of diminishing boundaries; it extends as far as its language reaches and its tools are used.

The third grade of morality is the human. Ordinarily a morality is society-wide, but it is also restricted. Its code belongs to a particular society whose members usually can conceive of no other. Yet there is in fact a different morality for each society, and, beyond each, there is one which belongs to the whole of humanity and so takes precedence over all others.

Individual man belongs to humanity in virtue of being human. It is something he *is* and it remains unaffected by what he *does,* an inescapable condition of his being. Many elements of morality cut across all particular societies, all special moralities. Heroic man is the same in all societies; so is the populist. Each special type has its own kind of connection.

The individual is always part of a society whose membership is finite. How many individuals are there? How many have there been? How many are there yet to be? All belong to the species and share a common humanity. This provides the basis for another level of responsibility. The individual exists among other individuals in virtue of those of his fellows who are not present and with whom through the species he is associated in a common humanity. From this connection a broader morality emerges.

What behavior does the morality of humanity call out in the individual? For one thing, in his conduct toward his society he must always take into consideration its effects upon other societies. Put otherwise, when an individual deals with his society he must always remember its relation to other societies.

This is the theory of confrontation, and it means that *the individual in every one of his thoughts, feelings and actions is confronted by the entire human species* and not merely by some special part of it. What individuals have in common at the deepest level is their humanity.

The fourth, and final, grade of morality is the cosmic. By the cosmos I mean of course the universe — with all that it is and all that it contains, all material objects and energies in space and time, all particles, all events, together with all possibilities, in short what in an earlier chapter was covered by the term "nature."

What is the cosmic good? The good is a quality, we must not

forget that, and the cosmic good is a world-quality, for all intrinsic good is cosmic good, the equality which prevails between any two things, a universal principle of moral gravitation, a beautiful symmetry of goods in which the ultimate reaches of morality are present in every instance of the good.

It is here that the urge of the individual to exceed himself turns toward the good: excessive behavior, with exaggerated good and bad effects. The urge to exceed himself accounts for all that is wonderful and terrible in human life. His monumental effort to become one with the source of his feelings of sublimity is his final responsibility. It can move him, however, in one of two oppposite ways. The spectacle of the sun led Plotinus to mystical flights of religious ecstasy in solitude. But it led the Aztecs to the ritual performance of the bloodiest of human sacrifices.

The word "species" has a wide application. It is not limited to animal species or even to organic species, it refers to all things in their kinds. Given the range of cosmic morality, all species are involved.

Responsibility at the cosmic level means that *the individual exists in virtue of those members of other species which do not and for which through his own species he is responsible*. Cosmic confrontation, then, means *conduct toward a particular species in consideration of all others*.

The outstanding fact about the cosmos is that there is no simple cosmic order similar to what is found in any social order. The cosmos is a mixture of order and disorder. If order is defined as similarity among differences, then disorder is the extent to which the elements of a given order are distributed outside that order among the elements of other orders. In this sense the distinction between order and disorder at the cosmic level breaks down, and cosmos and chaos are names for the same set of conditions.

Yet nature as a whole has its moral code. Everything at some time and place comes into existence and at another goes out of it. The moral life at the cosmic level means for the individual at some point surrendering his hold upon existence, or, as the Greek philospher, Anaximander, called it, "paying the penalty for injustice according to the ordering of time."

Human Nature at the Brink

To some of my readers it may seem that I have strayed from my original intention, which was to portray human nature. This is not the case. Human nature — the nature of the individual — is a deeper and more complex affair than any casual examination may reveal. Once you grant that the individual is a product of generations and that he could not survive alone, the rest follows.

No doubt every individual has his own arrangement of values, which differ even though not greatly from those of his neighbors. He also occupies a place slightly different from theirs because he has his own corner and consequently his own perspective. Any account of human nature must include the fact of his uniqueness, however much he is subject to uniformity in most matters. Nevertheless he must join with his contemporaries in the place they share in history.

In the great periods of civilization no one looks back. The ancient Greeks never collected antiques; the Romans did.

What are the prospects for mankind? Certain indications give hints. The saving element in the account is that nearly all projections prove to be wrong.

The effects of progress in material culture are sure to be determinative. When there were few men on earth they survived by adapting themselves to the environment; now that there are so many they can survive only by adapting the environment to themselves. Thus far no genetic changes have been detected as a result, but evolution is a slow process. For one thing, the life expectancy in scientific-industrial cultures has been doubled; but there are serious disabilities.

Human nature stands at the brink because men can neither accept nor reject what is facing them. They are never so happy as when enjoying the use of an out-of-date artifact, a sailboat or a horse and buggy; but it is the new artifacts which govern their behavior.

In a scientific-industrial culture such as our own most people have turned aside from the complex novelties that surround them and make no effort to understand. The familiar household objects, like telephones and television sets, are strange territory to those who benefit most from them, to say nothing of the new nuclear industry that produces the power to light and heat their homes. This is a new and uncomfortable kind of ignorance. What are people to do in such a case?

Equally important is the fact that in fitting them to live in modern cities technology has unfitted them to return to the primitive conditions of their remote ancestors. Recently some people have rejected civilization with all its disabilities to return to "a state of nature" as they supposed it to have been. They tried living in the woods without artifacts, but that was a failure. It cannot be done; man is not the same creature he was. On the other hand, how long can he sustain the high stage of technology he has succeeded in attaining? For how many centuries will the jumbo jets fly? If a species develops by adaptation to its environment, what will happen when the human species adapts to its artificial environment? We have seen that there is little in man's surroundings that is naturally occurring any longer now that the air he breathes has been purified, the land he walks on paved, the water he drinks filtered. Already the airplane and automobile have so conditioned him that he can no longer run as fast as the early American plains Indian.

Mankind has been woven more tightly into the environment. It is sometimes doubtful whether an artifact is part of the environment or part of a man: it stands half way between them. A book is a part of the environment, certainly, but what about an artificial hand? Or a pacemaker for the heart?

I see no harm in saying that man is a machine. If the machine seems inhuman, so is a man who has only one idea and can perform only one kind of operation, the victim of monomania, for instance. Nobody yet understands all the things a complex machine could do. Some machines are so intelligent they can be described as non-living individuals. Where does one leave off and the other begin?

The Control of the Future

If we extend this line of thought into the future, we see that life need no longer be accidental and unplanned, as it has been. There are three definite, distinctively different ways in which man may affect his future: by social engineering, by genetic engineering, and by environmental engineering.

The behavioristic psychologists and the neurophysiologists have devised a procedure by which human behavior may be predicted and controlled. It involves the use of positive and negative reinforcers in much the same way that laboratory animals are now manipulated.

Western civilization has reached a dangerous and critical stage. It has demonstrated by many internecine wars and conflicts that it contains elements which make it undesirable as a candidate for the role of global civilization. Would this not be equally true of all other candidates? Consider those small laboratories of civilization, the primitive cultures. Some have developed one side of human nature to the exclusion of others. To consider two recently discovered examples, the Ik represent the aggressive, destructive side; the Tasaday represent the opposite. The Ik hate everyone, including the members of their own group. The Tasaday seem to be lacking in all aggression.

Every individual loves and hates. It would be hard to imagine a society in which these two conflicting features of human nature were not contained; a global society would be no exception. It is possible that, due to the increase in populations and the complexity and power of artifacts, including of course nuclear weapons, the rhythm of war and peace may be ended suddenly by a single great conflict.

We have already noted that the basic cause of conflict is that ambivalence of aggression which lies deep within the organic needs of the body. That is the cause; there is seldom any difficulty in fixing on an occasion. Differences of any sort serve equally as a pretext; the commonest are differences in economic systems, in religious beliefs, and in ideas. Men do not feel secure or comfortable unless they are able to conduct their lives in terms of some absolute belief, which seems to most of them to be a necessity. Unfortunately, absolute beliefs are derived from some characteristic of group differences. Historically the most familiar are religious beliefs, which, when they lost their force, were replaced by nationalistic beliefs or by those based on economic class differences. The secularization of humanity has not resulted, as so many thought that it would, in drawing diverse peoples together, but in substituting a social in place of a supernatural ground for their differences. So long as the differences are the basis of absolute beliefs there will be wars.

Thanks to the sudden acceleration in technology, the decision-making process has moved forward. Man has been handed over to his own responsibility. Will he meet it inadvertently by using a series of nuclear explosions to control the population explosion? A frightful prospect but a genuine possibility.

The survival of mankind in the future depends upon getting free of the need for absolute belief or finding a basis for it in the similarities of peoples. There are no races of man (except in the trivial sense), there are only ideas and the people who hold them.

Perhaps the influence that counts for the most is the differences in ideas. Some people are united by the common acceptance of a set of ideas, others are separated by differences. All men live from day to day in the grip of some system of ideas. While some societies have been known to live only for their beliefs, others have gladly died for theirs. As soon as the connections between men and ideas is more widely recognized and appreciated, the conflicts between societies may lose some of their deadly force, and humanity will come together in harmony, as indeed its common origins and common fate suggest that it should.

* * *

The second way in which man can affect his own future is through genetic engineering.

Thanks to the latest development, named "recombinant DNA," biologists now possess the necessary technology to make alterations in any animal species, including the human. The process begins with the discovery of a class of enzymes used by bacteria to recognize and destroy foreign DNA. Known as restriction enzymes, they serve as a scissors-and-paste kit at the gene level. They can cut DNA molecules at sequences that occur a few genes apart, leaving them with sticky ends and allowing a genetic segment from one organism to be joined to a similarly cut segment from another, producing a hybrid molecule and thus a different organism.

This raises an interesting question. Now that we possess the technology for changing human nature, it is entirely practical to ask, *what kind of animal do we want to become?* Do we know? I think that for the moment we do not, but facing it involves a crucial decision. It is primarily a moral question and so the moralists must address themselves to finding an adequate answer.

* * *

The third way in which man can affect his own future is by environmental engineering.

If it is true that all animals adapt to their environment and therefore that man will have to adapt to his artificial environment, then it is up to him to determine what he will become by designing that environment so that it produces the desired effects on him. In other words, man has the power now to change the environment in such a way as to bring about the desired changes in himself. Individuals reflect their surroundings, and man's reactions to the right kind of environment would be more favorable to his aspirations. I take it that all artifacts are disturbances of nature, indeed all civilizations are; and so they must be of the right kind. But what exactly is "the right kind"? Perhaps we can fall back at this point on a simple principle: *all alterations in the environment must be made as closely as possible in conformity with an undisturbed nature.*

Thus far man's efforts in this direction have been negative: he has undertaken to restrict pollution, a necessary step. But there is also the problem of positive design. He can move to this next step of course only after he has decided what he wants his successors to be.

It is not difficult to guess what form it will take. The individual will have to be programmed to act on something less than absolute belief: namely, on the basis of a system of ideas held tentatively and always subject to revision when its premises are discovered to be either false, conflicting or incomplete. A flexible program of this sort could only come from adopting an open system, one based on probabilities rather than absolutes.

* * *

Until that far-off day when belief and truth are one and the same, there can be no peace on earth. In the meanwhile there are many absolute beliefs and they conflict, and men are willing to kill for them.

The individual contains far more cravings within him than he recognizes. We have noted that to effect a total reduction in all of his needs he would have to include and control all of the universe and what is more: identify with its maker. He may think of himself as something separate and unique, a product of his times. He is that, too, but he is also a product of history and contains within himself the provisions for what is to come. He inherits the past; he has linkages to the present in every direction, with everything in the universe as well as everybody in his own generation; and he helps to prepare mankind for the future.

Chapter XI
Life as a Stage Process

I began this book by talking about the needs of the individual, needs which come from organs of the body when they lack something. Then I went on to argue that in the drives to reduce these needs the individual gets involved with social groups, with artifacts, with institutions, with societies and states, with entire cultures, and finally with civilizations.

I tried throughout to keep the single individual in the foreground and to discuss the rest only in order to show how far into the complexities of his environment his needs took him. The individual in all this was a sort of dummy figure and a static affair. We all know that this is not the case. And so in this last chapter I want to return to him and consider the stages of his development from his birth to his death.

The Age Grades

We tend to think of the human individual, once he has become an adult, as an unchanging whole, entertaining the same views and living the same life so long as he is in full possession of his faculties. This does not check with the facts. Development consists in moving in time abruptly from one plateau to another, a move in which in each instance there is both a gain and a loss. In the account of the development of a single individual from his conception to his death, the details do not describe a continuous flow but, like life itself, a series of sharp changes, of conditions prevailing at various age-grades. Yet whether it is of the individual or of the species, the development itself never stops.

Every age-grade presents its own challenge which the individuals of that age must meet, and the challenge of each age-grade is of course different from those of the others. Life may be seen as a pattern, consisting in a series of passages in time from one stage to another. We tend to think of these as marking growth from conception to maturity, and decline from maturity to death. In advanced civilizations not all such passages are indicated by ceremonies, or formally acknowledged as they are in more primitive societies; though some still are in ours, as for instance birth, marriage and death. It is these distinct stages I wish to examine.

Living means an unfolding of personality so far as circumstances permit. But circumstances, if one takes the longest view of the time during which they have been operating, determine the personality in the first place. As Whitman wrote in his "Song of Myself", "Before I was born out of my mother generations guided me"; generations which had interacted with the environment and been changed by it; everything that comes into existence in the external world must first emerge from it. The individual goes through the same stages as those of any other organism. He emerges from the past, and helps to prepare for the future; the life of man has a direction: it is indicated by the arrow of time.

In this sense everything is inherently intentional, and life at any given stage is lived in accordance with it. The happiness of childhood, the hope of youth, the activity of maturity, the wisdom of middle age, the resignation of senescence; these phrases refer to personal outlooks and perspective states. The intentional consciousness is only the reflective and aware side of the organism; where the whole organism is intentional, every part of it is also.

The individual is an intentional entity, poised for change and pointed in the way indicated by the time categories; time, so to speak, made self-aware. Man is the only animal aware of the flow of time and this endows him with a special responsibility. The consciousness of existence is also the conscience of existence; the elements which characterize all of existence are raised to the level of self-awareness. What the human individual knows that he is, is what other kinds of animals are without their knowledge. Thus man has a responsibility for the rest of existence in representing it.

In human life, a journey marked by abrupt transitional stages, the rites of passage: birth, coming-of-age, marriage, death, are, as van Gennep pointed out, ways of recognizing the necessity to control definite changes because of the danger inherent in them. The social recognition of these changes is also a taming of the power suddenly involved. Every new stage is a regeneration, a renewed force and also a different force, involving a fresh outlook and altered interests. Society is not merely a collection of individuals but also a page from the volume of nature, torn out, so to speak, and separated from the rest. This is recognized in the sacred as distinct from the profane character of things and events.

Thus it is that the rites of passage are also connected with the seasons of the year. A child is born, but according to the vegetative cycle so is nature in the spring; an old man dies, but so does nature in the fall.

There is no adequate preparation at one stage of life for the next. Each has its own authority; the transitions are definite. When the human individual becomes adjusted to one kind of existence and finds himself able to meet its demands and derive from it some of its benefits, he is catapulted into another kind and confronted with an altogether new set of conditions which he is unprepared to deal with. If he is to survive and flourish anew, he will have to make rapid and adequate accommodations to them. He was a child? He is an adolescent. He was a youth? Suddenly he is a mature adult. He had established himself in middle age? It is removed and he has turned into an old man, incapacitated for dealing with most happenings. The development of the individual consists in a series of seemingly permanent stages and of sudden drops into new conditions bringing new experience with no time for preparation.

The age-grades are a series of plateaus, each of which looks out upon an indefinitely extended and monotonous vista, from which it can be falsely concluded only that things have always been and always will be the same. There is in the individual a memory for facts but not for emotions. It is not easy and in most cases not even possible for the individual to recall how he felt upon some previous occasion in his distant past. By "distant" here need only be meant "in some previous age-grade."

It is impossible for the individual to anticipate how he will feel on some future occasion if it is to occur at a different age-grade. Communications between people of different age-grades is difficult, and cannot be established in any complete sense. When individuals operate from different principles, they rarely come to the same conclusions; and this is reflected in the qualities of their feelings as much as it is in the meanings of their thoughts.

Among the many distinguishing features of the world confronting the slowly awakening individual, two of the sharpest and most insistent are: the similarities which connect things and the differences which separate them. Space and time furnish the arena for comparison, so that even those things which are similar are also separated.

The individual, in his attempt to understand the nature of the world which is to be the scene of his struggles for need-reduction through the drives, is compelled to order what he knows of that world.

A Philosophy of Life

A belief about the world is a practical tool, for it orients the individual through all his strivings, which is why it comes about that everyone has a philosophy, recognized or not. He needs it if he is to maintain his sanity, which depends upon his knowledge of his place in the scheme of things.

Every such philosophy is true to the extent to which it is consistent, and inclusive to the extent to which it represents the external world in which the individual lives. Such truth as it has is apt to be in what it affirms, though not all that it affirms is true; and such falsity in what it denies, though not all its denials are false.

The individual may not be aware that he has a personal philosophy of life, because it lies at a deep level in him, which makes it all the more powerful. The more profound his beliefs the more consistent his actions. His philosophy is called a philosophy of life because he lives by it; and it is personal because to some extent it is his alone. It may be defined as a system of beliefs about the world and his place in it. As he develops and changes, so also does his philosophy. The same truth does not appear the same from the different perspectives of age-grades. If for instance it is true that activity is as much a source of reliable knowledge as thought and feeling are, this is not a truth which will appeal as much to the old as it does to the young. The old who accept it will view it with sadness; the young will grasp it eagerly and be anxious to put it into practice.

There is no consistency among the philosophies implied at every stage in an individual's life. The rites of passage from one age-grade to another are also those from one philosophy to another. At first with only a faint suggestion of consistency indicated by the individual's needs and actions, his philosophy develops into a full-blown and largely organized doctrine, maintained by others as a system of beliefs.

The professional philosophers have thought of their philosophies as competing, so that if one were true the others must be false. That is not the opinion I maintain. I believe that philosophies which are different, as different, say, as Plato's and Hegel's, or as Kant's and Aristotle's, owe their difference to the fact that because their observations were made from highly diverse positions, their conclusions appear to be opposed. No two philosophies can be wholly true, but then probably no one philosophy is, either. It is possible to reconcile partial truths derived from narrow and limited outlooks; and narrow and limited is what any finite outlook must necessarily be.

I hold that the great philosophers were in the main true in what they affirmed and false in what they denied. If their followers were willing to forego their absolute claims, not only could the limited truths of each and all be defended, but, more importantly for practice, each could be maintained as particularly suitable to the individual as determined by his stage of life.

Philosophies being partial affairs may be assigned to various periods in the lifetime of the single individual according to what he might be inclined to believe naturally at his age-grade. It seems as likely for a man as he matures to slip out of one philosophy and into another as it is for him to put away childish things and assume the responsibilities of an adult. As he passes through different stages and has different adventures, so also he must be experiencing different moods. Since each philosophy is a partial truth, there being as yet no philosophy which is at once capable of expressing the whole of truth in all its details, then for each stage in the development of the individual there must be a philosophy appropriate both to his understanding and his moods. Philosophy, whether of the intuitive or systematic variety, whether for example, like Nietzsche's or like Kant's, is mood music.

The reason for assigning a philosophy to each of the age-groups is that all philosophies are to some extent true. Each is a limited and partial view of reality, where "reality" is understood as the immediate object of that which is true. Age-grades necessarily provide the same kind of limited views, each partly true.

Thus while traditional philosophies are logically in conflict, it can be seen that they meet and supplement each other when they are considered in connection with the age-grades. Thus it is legitimate to speak of Heideggerian gestation, Humean infancy, Husserlian childhood, Herbartian early school years, Schopenhauerian adolescence, Cartesian youth, Deweyan manhood, Aristotelian and Hegelian maturity, Stoic later middle age, Bergsonian and Heraclitean old age, and Kierkegaardian senescence.

The search made by each individual for the understanding of the material world by which he is surrounded is the search also for completeness, which is in the end the search of each man for himself, externally expressed. The individual is the representative of his species, and there is not so much divergence between individuals that it is inaccurate to say that any one bent on reducing his needs is after all only one example of mankind.

Suggestions for Further Reading

Chapter I

BY WAY OF INTRODUCTION

Bertrand Russell, *A History of Western Philosophy* (New York 1945, Simon and Schuster).

Discussions of the three thinkers mentioned in this chapter and their views of human nature.

Chapter II

THE TOTAL ENVIRONMENT

Kees Boeke, *Cosmic View* (New York, no date, The John Day Company).

An extraordinarily clever view of the natural world taken from the human perspective. The progressive levels of things smaller than man, then the corresponding levels larger. Highly recommended.

Chapter III

THE ORIGIN OF THE INDIVIDUAL AS A BUNDLE OF NEEDS

Marston Bates, *Man in Nature* (Englewood Cliffs, New Jersey 1961, Prentice-Hall).

A good brief account of man's development and his place in the world.

James K. Feibleman, *Mankind Behaving:* Human Needs and Material Culture (Springfield, Ill. 1963, Charles C. Thomas).

A broad theory of human motivation for the general understanding of why individuals act in the way that they do.

R. J. Forbes, *Man the Maker* (New York 1950, Henry Schuman).

The development of man in relation to his tools.

C. Judson Herrick, *The Evolution of Human Nature* (Austin, Texas 1956, University of Texas Press).

John Lewis, *Man and Evolution* (London 1962, Lawrence and Wishart).

M. F. Ashley Montagu (ed.), *Culture: Man's Adaptive Dimension* (New York 1968, Oxford University Press).

Three good general accounts of human evolution.

Chapter IV

IMMEDIATE SURVIVAL AND THE SHORT-RANGE SELF

Bernal Diaz del Castillo, *Conquest of New Spain*

The classic contemporary account by an eye-witness in

1521 of widespread cannibalism among the Aztecs.

Jean-Pierre Hallet, *Congo Kitabu* (New York 1966, Random House).

Two accounts of cannibalism in contemporary Africa.

D. O. Hebb, *A Textbook of Psychology* (Philadelphia 1958, W. B. Saunders).

Though perhaps somewhat out of date, the best account I have found of physiological psychology.

Piers Paul Read, *Alive* (New York 1974, J. B. Lippincott).

A recent instance of cannibalism provoked by circumstances.

Chapter V

ULTIMATE SURVIVAL AND THE LONG-RANGE SELF

John C. Eccles, *The Understanding of the Brain* (New York 1973).

As much as we know about the brain at the present time. Very good about the connections between the brain and languages.

Konrad Lorenz, *On Aggression* (New York 1963, Harcourt Brace and World).

Aggression in animals and what it may tell us about the human animal.

P. B. Medawar, *The Uniqueness of The Individual* (New York 1957, Basic Books).

The skin as an organ of uniqueness. Also many excellent observations on the peculiarities of man as a biological species.

Chapter VI

THE NEEDS IN GENERAL

Douglas K. Candland (ed.), *Emotion: Bodily Change* (New York 1962, D. Van Nostrand).

Sir Charles Sherrington, *The Integrative Action of The Nervous System* (New Haven 1947, Yale University Press).

Includes a good brief account of older theories of the emotions.

Chapter VII

THE SOCIAL ENVIRONMENT

Emile Durkheim, *The Division of Labor,* G. Simpson, trans. (Glencoe, Ill. 1949, Free Press).

James K. Feibleman, *The Institutions of Society* (New York 1968, Humanities Press).

Geraint Perry, *Political Elites* (London 1969, Allen and Unwin).

Rupert Wilkinson (ed.), *Governing Elites* (New York 1969, Oxford University Press).

Two little known studies but good ones of the personnel of leading institutions.

Chapter VIII

THE DOMAIN OF INSTITUTIONS

Abram Tertz (Andrei Sinyavsky), *A Voice from The Chorus* (New York 1976, Farrar, Straus and Giroux).

An account of Soviet prisons by a dissident writer who later emigrated to France.

Harry Woolf (ed.), *Science As A Cultural Force* (Baltimore 1964, Johns Hopkins Press).

Chapter IX

THE DOMAIN OF CULTURES

Ruth Benedict, *Patterns of Culture* (Boston 1934, Houghton Mifflin).

The classical account of the diversity of cultures, with good examples from primitive societies.

James K. Feibleman, *The Theory of Human Culture* (New York 1968, Humanities Press).

Broad consideration of what constitutes a culture, with special reference to the role in it of the single human individual.

C. H. Waddington, *The Ethical Animal* (London 1960, Allen and Unwin).

An excellent account of the relation of man to his material culture.

From Max Weber: Essays in Sociology, H. H. Gerth and C. Wright Mills (eds.), (New York 1946, Oxford University Press).

Selection of the work of a great thinker in sociology, one who was especially concerned with problems involving the state, bureaucracy and religion.

Chapter X

THE GLOBAL ENVIRONMENT

James K. Feibleman, *Moral Strategy* (The Hague 1967, Martinus Nijhoff).

A fuller treatment of the moral outcome.

Jane M. Murphy, "Psychiatric Labeling in Cross-Cultural Perspective", *Science*, 191, 1019-1028, 1976.

> An excellent description of the occurrence of the same mental illnesses in many cultures.

John Nance, *The Gentle Tasaday* (New York 1977, Harcourt Brace Jovanovich).

> An account of a people who would not hurt anything or anybody.

Carl Sagan, *The Cosmic Connection* (New York 1973, Doubleday).

> An admirable survey of the prospect of life elsewhere in the universe.

Colin M. Turnbull, *The Mountain People* (New York 1972, Simon and Schuster).

> An account of the Ik, who loathe everyone including themselves.

Chapter XI

LIFE AS A STAGE PROCESS

James K. Feibleman, *The Stages of Human Life* (The Hague 1975, Martinus Nijhoff).

Arnold van Jennep, *The Rites of Passage*, M. B. Vizedom and G. L. Caffee, trans. (Chicago 1960, University Press).

Index